Social Issues
in Literature

Democracy in the Poetry of Walt Whitman

Other Books in the Social Issues in Literature Series:

Social Issues in Literature

Democracy in the Poetry of Walt Whitman

Thomas Riggs and Company, Book Editors

GREENHAVEN PRESS
A part of Gale, Cengage Learning

GALE
CENGAGE Learning

Detroit • New York • San Francisco • New Haven, Conn • Waterville, Maine • London

GALE
CENGAGE Learning

Elizabeth Des Chenes, *Director, Publishing Solutions*

© 2013 Greenhaven Press, a part of Gale, Cengage Learning

Gale and Greenhaven Press are registered trademarks used herein under license.

For more information, contact:
Greenhaven Press
27500 Drake Rd.
Farmington Hills, MI 48331-3535
Or you can visit our Internet site at gale.cengage.com

For product information and technology assistance, contact us at

Gale Customer Support, 1-800-877-4253
For permission to use material from this text or product, submit all requests online at www.cengage.com/permissions

Further permissions questions can be emailed to permissionrequest@cengage.com

Articles in Greenhaven Press anthologies are often edited for length to meet page requirements. In addition, original titles of these works are changed to clearly present the main thesis and to explicitly indicate the author's opinion. Every effort is made to ensure that Greenhaven Press accurately reflects the original intent of the authors. Every effort has been made to trace the owners of copyrighted material.

Cover image © Classic Image/Alamy.

LIBRARY OF CONGRESS CATALOGING-IN-PUBLICATION DATA

Democracy in the poetry of Walt Whitman / Thomas Riggs and company, book editors.
    p. cm. -- (Social issues in literature)
  Includes bibliographical references and index.
  ISBN 978-0-7377-6377-5 (hardcover) -- ISBN 978-0-7377-6378-2 (pbk.)
  1. Whitman, Walt, 1819-1892--Criticism and interpretation. 2. Whitman, Walt, 1819-1892--Political and social views. 3. Democracy in literature.
  4. Riggs, Thomas, 1963-
  PS3242.P64D46 2012
  811'.3--dc23
                                                                    2012015513

Printed in the United States of America
2 3 4 5 6   20 19 18 17 16

Contents

Chapter 1: Background on Walt Whitman

Whitman began his career as a somewhat traditional writer of fiction and editorials but underwent a transformation in the late 1840s that caused him to develop the distinctive free-verse style of *Leaves of Grass* and the patriotic tone of *Drum-Taps*.

Whitman's appreciation of the common individual stems from his honest examination of the successes and failures of American democracy, not from a naive spirituality or mysticism.

Although Whitman was a champion of the average citizen throughout his life, his positions in relation to issues such as slavery, women's suffrage, and the role of the federal government were far more complex than is often assumed.

Chapter 2: Democracy in Walt Whitman's Poetry

Generations of poets after Whitman drew inspiration from his ability to fuse political ideals with expressive language. Writers of the early twentieth century eschewed his dependence on plain language but employed a variety of styles to make their works more democratic.

Whitman is typically characterized as a champion of democracy, but his contradictory views about slavery, race, and homosexuality indicate otherwise.

Chapter 3: Contemporary Perspectives on Democracy

Introduction

Walt Whitman is often referred to as the father of American poetry, and for good reason: His work embodies the seemingly incompatible cross-currents of American political thought. As the author of the notorious "Song of Myself," Whitman celebrates the rugged individualism and stoic self-reliance that would later give rise to the myth of the lonesome American cowboy making his way westward through inhospitable terrain, surviving on his wits and brute strength alone. As the author of "Democratic Vistas," Whitman is a champion of collectivism—the concern for the universal safety and well-being of every citizen, regardless of social status, and the willingness to make personal sacrifices to ensure that safety and well-being. Whitman's achievement was not that he grasped the importance of these philosophical positions in the grand experiment of American democracy but that he was able to see them as complementary rather than mutually exclusive components of the ideal society.

During Whitman's lifetime, however, the fate of democracy in America was very much in doubt. The American and French Revolutions of the late eighteenth century had initiated a shift of power from the elite few (i.e., the aristocracy) to the many. Whitman shaped his poetic style to reflect changing social ideals, rejecting traditional poetic forms and language in favor of a new, conversational form of poetry that was designed to be accessible to the common reader rather than just the learned elite. But as the nineteenth century wore on, people began to question who exactly benefited from this changing power structure. In America, wealthy, white male landowners enjoyed numerous freedoms that were denied to other significant segments of the population, especially slaves and women. The rise of the abolitionist and woman's suffrage movements brought such inequalities to the forefront of public attention. By the presidential election of 1860, a proposed federal mandate to end slavery throughout the nation initiated a political firestorm that threatened to tear apart the very fabric of the American experiment. Following the election of Abraham Lincoln as the sixteenth president of the United States, seven southern states announced their secession from the Union, marking the start of the Civil War.

At its core, the Civil War exemplified the uneasy relationship between America's individualist and collectivist impulses. The Confederates and their supporters felt that individual states had the right to determine their own stance on issues such as slavery without interference from the federal government, while President Lincoln and the Unionists believed it was the government's duty to ensure that the entire nation lived up to its credo that "all men are created equal." As David S. Reynolds and others note in this volume, Whitman's sympathies did not rest easily with either camp. Though he was a vehement supporter of the Union, writing patriotic poems and even serving as a volunteer nurse during the war, he was distrustful of overeducated government officials and wary of civil rights groups' tendency to disrupt social harmony. But it was his unwavering belief in the infinite potential of the individual, as well as his vision of America as a collection of diverse individuals working in unison to usher in a new era of spiritual enlightenment and personal liberty, that drove him to become a vocal supporter of the Union cause.

Nineteenth-century reviewers of Whitman's poetry, especially those from the Confederate states, often ridiculed him as a naive idealist who refused to recognize what they saw as a natural division between races, genders, and social classes. In the twentieth century, however, several scholars noted that Whitman's work prior to the 1855 publication of *Leaves of Grass* contains passages that seem to support slavery and reveal fundamentally undemocratic and racist attitudes. The truth lies somewhere in between. Whitman's worldview was never static; it evolved over time, as evidenced by the numerous editions and revisions of *Leaves of Grass* that he published throughout his life. He viewed American democracy as a similarly unfinished project, a work-in-progress that must be continually shaped by the collective efforts of empowered individuals from all walks of life. Such foresight leads modern critics to regard Whitman as one of the few American poets of the nineteenth century whose work remains as relevant and thought provoking today as it was when written. Many commentators point to the fierce debates surrounding the responsibility of the public to sustain a social safety net through tax-funded programs such as social security, unemployment insurance, and Medicare as an extension of the complex issues that Whitman engaged in his writings. And, while he provides no concrete suggestions to settle the debate, the Good Gray Poet depicts the promise and potential of democracy in America with such vitality that he continues to inspire readers to recognize their own ability to "contain multitudes."

Chronology

1819

Walter Whitman is born on May 31 in West Hills, Long Island, the second of eight children of Walter and Louisa Van Velsor Whitman.

1823

The Whitman family moves to Brooklyn, New York.

1830

Whitman is taken out of school by his father in order to help support the family.

1831

Whitman begins to apprentice as a printer for various New York newspapers.

1833

The Whitman family returns to Long Island, but Whitman stays in New York City.

1836

Whitman joins his family on Long Island and begins working as a teacher.

1838

Whitman attempts to establish his own newspaper, the *Long Islander*, but the venture fails, and he returns to teaching.

1840

Whitman starts to write fiction, and over the next several years he has a number of stories published in various periodicals, including the *Democratic Review*.

1841
Whitman moves back to New York City.

1842
Whitman works as a journalist on a number of New York newspapers, including the *New York Sunday Times* and *New York Statesman*. He serves as editor of the *New York Aurora* and the *Evening Tattler*. In November his temperance novel, *Franklin Evans; or the Inebriate*, is published as a supplement to the *New World*.

1845
Whitman relocates to Brooklyn and begins writing for the *Long Island Star*.

1846
In March Whitman becomes editor of the *Brooklyn Daily Eagle*, a position he holds until January 1848, when a political disagreement with the newspaper's owner leads to Whitman's departure.

1848
Whitman moves to New Orleans to start the *New Orleans Daily Crescent* newspaper for owner J.E. McClure but stays for only a few months before returning to New York.

1850
Whitman enters a period of soul searching and reading and writing, while working odd jobs.

1855
Whitman self-publishes the first edition of *Leaves of Grass*, which contains twelve untitled poems. Whitman's father dies on July 11.

1856
Whitman publishes the second edition of *Leaves of Grass*, which has thirty-two poems. It is not well received by the literary community.

1857

Whitman, financially strapped and the main provider for his family, becomes editor of the *Brooklyn Daily Times*, a position he holds until his dismissal in 1859.

1860

The third edition of *Leaves of Grass*, featuring new and revised poems, is published by Boston publishing firm Thayer and Eldridge.

1861

Whitman writes about city life and the social impact of the Civil War in articles for the *Brooklyn Standard*.

1862

Whitman travels to Virginia to find his brother George, who has been wounded in the Civil War.

1863

Whitman moves to Washington, D.C., and finds work as a government clerk. He also volunteers as a nurse to help wounded soldiers.

1865

Whitman becomes a government clerk for the Department of the Interior's Indian Bureau division. *Drum-Taps*, a collection of fifty-three poems, is published by Peter Eckler, followed shortly after by *Sequel to Drum-Taps*.

1867

The fourth edition of *Leaves of Grass* is published.

1870

Whitman publishes the fifth edition of *Leaves of Grass* as well as *Democratic Vistas* and *Passage to India* (although all three are dated 1871).

1873
After suffering a stroke, Whitman takes a leave from his government post and relocates to Camden, New Jersey, to live with his brother George.

1874
Whitman loses his government clerkship.

1876
The sixth edition of *Leaves of Grass*, which offers no new material, is published along with a companion volume titled *Two Rivulets*.

1881
The seventh edition of *Leaves of Grass* is published by respected publisher James R. Osgood.

1882
The seventh edition of *Leaves of Grass* is banned in Boston due to its sexual content. It is republished by a number of other publishers, including Rees Welsh of Philadelphia.

1892
Whitman dies on March 26.

Background on
Walt Whitman

The Life of Walt Whitman

Ed Folsom and Kenneth M. Price

Dictionary of Literary Biography *is a specialist encyclopedia devoted to literature and published by the Gale Group.*

In the following biographical essay, Folsom and Price survey several crucial moments in Walt Whitman's development as one of the most important poets in American history. Whitman's concern with social issues such as the abolition of slavery and gender equality heavily influenced his professional and literary demeanor as he railed against perceived injustices in editorials, fictional pieces, and short poems throughout the 1840s. In his groundbreaking poetry collection Leaves of Grass *(1855), he abandoned conventional poetic techniques for a looser, more conversational form of poetry featuring a robust "I" persona. The social tumult of the Civil War provided Whitman an opportunity to connect this new poetic identity with an evolving national identity in* Drum-Taps *(1865), and he became a stout defender of American democracy and working-class citizens in his later works* Democratic Vistas *(1871) and* Passage to India *(1871), making him a hero of social activists across several generations.*

Widely considered the most influential and innovative poet of America, Walt Whitman was born in West Hills, a village near Hempstead, Long Island, on 31 May 1819 to Walter and Louisa Van Velsor Whitman. . . .

Whitman's formal education consisted of six years in the Brooklyn public schools (which was far more schooling than either of his parents had received). At eleven he began work-

Ed Folsom and Kenneth M. Price, "Walt Whitman," in *Dictionary of Literary Biography: Antebellum Writers in New York*, vol. 250, no. 2, ed. Kent P. Ljungquist. Detroit: Gale Group, 2002, pp. 348–83. All rights reserved. Reproduced by permission.

ing as an office boy for some prominent Brooklyn lawyers; they gave him a subscription to a circulating library, where his self-education began. . . .

In the summer of 1831 Whitman became an apprentice printer on the *Long Island Patriot*, a liberal working-class newspaper in Brooklyn. He soon began contributing to the newspaper and experiencing the exhilaration of getting his own words published. . . .

By the time he was sixteen Whitman was a journeyman printer and compositor, working in various printing shops in New York City; he always retained a typesetter's concern for how his words looked on a page, the typeface in which they appeared, and the effects of various spatial arrangements. But then two of New York's worst fires wiped out the major printing and business centers of the city, and Whitman joined his family at Hempstead in 1836.

Rebelling at his father's attempts to get him to work on the new family farm. Whitman spent the next five years teaching school in at least ten Long Island towns. . . .

Early Fiction Writing

Whitman returned to New York City and began writing fiction. About twenty newspapers and magazines published his stories between 1840 and 1845. . . .

[In 1842] Park Benjamin, editor of the New York paper *The New World*, decided that Whitman was the perfect candidate to write a novel to capitalize on the booming temperance movement. . . .

Benjamin's *New World* published Whitman's *Franklin Evans; or The Inebriate: A Tale of the Times*, about a country boy who, after falling prey to drink in the big city, causes the deaths of three women. The work, in its fascination with "fatal pleasure," Evans's name for the strong attraction most men feel for sinful experience, be it drink or sex is typical of the temperance literature of the time in bringing in sensationalism under a moral guise. Whitman's treatment of sex, however, is unpersuasive and seems to confirm a remark he had made two years earlier: that he knew nothing about women either by "experience or observation." The novel is, nonetheless, one of the earliest explorations in American literature of the theme of miscegenation [interracial love]. It succeeded despite being a patched-together concoction of new writing and previously composed stories: around twenty thousand copies were sold—more than of anything else Whitman published in his lifetime. In his old age he described *Franklin Evans* to his friend Horace Traubel as "damned rot—rot of the worst sort" and claimed that he completed it in three days, composing some of it in the reading room of Tammany Hall, inspired by gin cocktails (on another occasion he said that he was buoyed by a bottle of port.). . .

In 1842–1843 Whitman, like many journalists of the period, moved in and out of positions on an array of newspapers. . . . His editorial topics ranged from criticism of police roundups of prostitutes to denunciation of Bishop John Hughes for trying to use public funds to support parochial schools.

Whitman left Manhattan in 1845 for steadier work in the somewhat less competitive journalistic environment of Brooklyn. . . .

Whitman was adamant in his editorials that slavery not be allowed into the new western territories, because he feared that whites would not migrate to areas where their labor was devalued by competition from slaves. He expressed outrage at practices that furthered slavery, such as laws that made possible the importation of slaves by way of Brazil. Like Abraham Lincoln, he consistently opposed slavery, even though he knew—again like Lincoln—that the more extreme abolitionists threatened the Union itself. He finally lost his position as editor of the [Brooklyn] *Eagle* because the publisher, Isaac Van Anden, sided with conservative proslavery Democrats.

This 1854 steel engraving of Walt Whitman in his thirties, created by Samuel Hollyer after a daguerreotype by photographer Gabriel Harrison, appeared opposite the title page in the 1855 first edition of Leaves of Grass. © Historical/Corbis.

On 9 February 1846 Whitman met J.E. McClure during intermission at the Broadway Theatre in New York. McClure and his partner, A.H. Hayes, were planning to launch a paper, the *Crescent*, in New Orleans. On the spot McClure hired Whitman to edit the paper and provided him with an advance to cover his travel expenses to New Orleans. Whitman's brother Jeff went with him to work as an office boy on the paper. The journey by train, steamboat, and stagecoach was Whitman's first excursion outside the New York City–Brooklyn–Long Island area. . . .

The *Crescent* owners exhibited what Whitman called a "singular sort of coldness" toward their new editor; they probably feared that he would embarrass them because of his unorthodox ideas, especially about slavery. Whitman's sojourn in New Orleans lasted only three months, but it produced a few lively sketches of life in the city and at least one poem. . . .

Transformation as a Poet

The mystery about Whitman in the late 1840s is the speed of his transformation from an unoriginal and conventional poet. He abruptly abandoned conventional rhyme and meter and began finding beauty in the commonplace but expressing it in an uncommon way. . . .

At this time of poetic transformation Whitman's politics—especially his racial attitudes—also underwent a profound alteration. Blacks become central to his poetry and to his understanding of democracy. . . .

His extreme political despair led him to replace what he named the "scum" of corrupt American politics in the 1850s with his own persona: a shaman, a culture healer, an all-encompassing "I."

That "I" became the main character of *Leaves of Grass*, the explosive book of twelve untitled poems that Whitman wrote in the early 1850s. . . .

Whitman later claimed that the first edition sold out, but, in fact, the sales were poor. He sent copies to several well-known writers—including John Greenleaf Whittier, who, legend has it, threw it into the fire—but the only one who responded was [Ralph Waldo] Emerson, who recognized in Whitman's work the spirit, tone, and style for which he had called. "I greet you at the beginning of a great career," Emerson wrote on 21 July, noting that *Leaves of Grass* "meets the demand I am always making of what seemed the sterile & stingy Nature, as if too much handiwork or too much lymph in the temperament were making our western wits fat & meat." Whitman's poetry, Emerson believed, would get the country into shape, helping to work off its excess of aristocratic fat. . . .

Whitman did not put his name on the title page of the book—an unconventional act suggesting that the author believed that he spoke not for himself but for America. (His name did not appear on a title page of *Leaves of Grass* until the 1876 "Author's Edition," and then only because he signed each copy as it was sold.) But opposite the title page was a portrait of Whitman, an engraving by Samuel Hollyer from a daguerreotype taken by the photographer Gabriel Harrison in the summer of 1854. The most famous frontispiece in literary history, it shows Whitman from head to just above the knees; he is dressed in workman's clothes, shirt open, hat cocked to the side, standing insouciantly and fixing the reader with a challenging stare. It is a pose that indicates Whitman's redefinition of the role of poet as the democratic spokesperson who no longer speaks only from the intellect and with the formality of tradition and education; the new poet pictured in Whitman's book speaks from and with the whole body and writes outside, in nature, not in the library. Whitman called his work "al fresco" poetry, indicating that it was written outside the bounds of convention and tradition.

Within a few months of the publication of the first edition of *Leaves of Grass* Whitman was at work on the second. . . .

In May 1857 Whitman went to work for the *Brooklyn Daily Times*, a Free Soil [a political party opposed to the expansion of slavery] newspaper; in the summer of 1859, once again, a disagreement with the newspaper's owner led to his dismissal. Meanwhile, he was forging literary connections. Emerson had come to visit at the end of 1855—they had gone back to

Emerson's room at the elegant Astor Hotel, where Whitman, dressed informality as in his frontispiece portrait, was denied admission. It was the first of many meetings the two men had over the next twenty-five years, as their relationship turned into one of grudging mutual respect mixed with suspicion. In 1856 Henry David Thoreau and Bronson Alcott visited Whitman's home; in his journal Alcott described Thoreau and Whitman as each "surveying the other curiously, like two beasts, each wondering what the other would do." Whitman . . . got to know several women's rights activists and feminist writers, some of whom became ardent readers and supporters. . . . Their radical ideas about sexual equality had a growing impact on Whitman's poetry. He also knew many abolitionist writers. . . .

A New Edition of *Leaves of Grass*

In February 1860 Whitman received a letter from William Thayer and Charles Eldridge, whose aggressive new Boston publishing house specialized in abolitionist literature; they wanted to publish the next edition of *Leaves of Grass*. Whitman readily agreed, and . . . traveled to Boston in March to oversee the printing. . . .

With the 1860 edition of *Leaves of Grass* Whitman began the incessant rearranging of his poems in various groupings that often alter their meaning and significance. . . .

The edition received many reviews, most of them positive—particularly those by women, who were more exhilarated than offended by Whitman's candid images of sex and the body and welcomed his attempt to sing "The Female equally with the male," as he put it in the poem "One's-Self I Sing." . . .

During the first year and a half of the Civil War, Whitman remained in the New York City area. . . . He had been visiting Broadway Hospital for several years, comforting injured stage drivers and ferryboat workers. . . .

As the Civil War began taking its toll, wounded soldiers joined the transportation workers as patients Whitman saw on his frequent rounds. The soldiers came from all over the country, and their reminiscences of home taught Whitman about the breadth and diversity of the growing nation. He developed an idiosyncratic style of informal personal nursing, writing down stories the patients told him, giving them small gifts, writing letters for them, and holding and kissing them. . . .

Move to Washington

In December 1862 the name "G.W. Whitmore" appeared in the newspaper casualty roster from Fredericksburg. Fearful that the name was a garbled version of George Washington Whitman, Whitman immediately set out for Virginia to try to find his brother. . . . After futilely searching for George in the nearly forty Washington hospitals, Whitman took a government boat and an army-controlled train to the battlefield at Fredericksburg to see if George was still there. He found George's unit and discovered that his brother had received only a superficial facial wound. But Whitman's relief turned to horror when, as he wrote in his journal, outside a mansion converted into a field hospital he came upon "a heap of amputated feet, legs, arms, hands, &c., a full load for a one-horse cart." . . .

It is not known when Whitman decided to stay in Washington, D.C. Like virtually all of the abrupt changes in his life—quitting teaching, going to New Orleans and to Boston, and, years later, deciding overnight to settle in Camden, New Jersey—this one came with no planning, advance notice, or preparation. . . .

[The decision] may have been made on the trip back to Washington in early January 1863, when he was put in charge of a trainload of casualties who were being transferred to hospitals in the capital. While the wounded were being moved to a steamboat for the trip up the Potomac, Whitman wandered among them, comforting them and writing down and promising to send their messages to their families. Perhaps by the time he got to Washington, determined to stay a few days to visit wounded soldiers from Brooklyn, he knew at some level that he would have to remain there for the duration of the war.

Whitman's Boston connections served him well in Washington: he got the letters of introduction from Emerson [that he had requested], a room in O'Connor's boardinghouse, and, through Eldridge, the publisher of the 1860 *Leaves of Grass* who was serving as assistant to the army paymaster, a part-time job as a copyist in the paymaster's office. . . .

The nation's capital was in a chaotic state in 1863, with unpaved streets and many half-completed government buildings, including the Capitol itself. Lincoln insisted that construction proceed at full pace, and some of the newly constructed buildings were almost immediately turned into hospitals. The U.S. Patent Office became a hospital in 1863, and Whitman noted the irony of the "rows of sick, badly wounded and dying soldiers" surrounding the "glass cases" displaying the inventions that had created modern warfare.

Whitman's job in the paymaster's office occasionally required him to go on trips to visit troops, as when he traveled to Analostan Island in July 1863 to help issue paychecks to the First Regiment U.S. Colored Troops. He was "well pleas'd" with their professional conduct and strong demeanor. . . . The war, for all of its destruction, was clearing the space for a broader American identity. . . .

Drum-Taps

After the burst of creativity in the mid and late 1850s that had resulted in the vastly expanded 1860 *Leaves of Grass*, Whitman had not written many poems until he got to Washington. There the daily encounters with soldiers opened a fresh vein of creativity that produced a poetry more modest in ambition and muted in its claims, a poetry in which death was no longer indistinguishable from life. . . . The poems were so different from any in *Leaves of Grass* that Whitman assumed that they could never be joined in the same book with the earlier ones, so he gathered them, along with the ones Thayer and Eldridge had planned to publish as "Banner at Day-Break," into a book he called *Drum-Taps*—the title evoking both the beating of the drums that accompanied soldiers into battle and the beating out of "Taps," the death march sounded at the burial of soldiers (originally played on the drums instead of the trumpet). . . .

During the early summer [of 1864] Whitman began to complain of a sore throat, dizziness, and a "bad feeling" in his head. Physician friends persuaded him to go back to Brooklyn for a rest. Whitman took the *Drum-Taps* manuscript with him, hoping to publish it while he was there.

In Brooklyn, Whitman could not stop doing what had become both a routine and a reason for his existence: he visited wounded soldiers in New York-area hospitals. . . .

[In early 1865 Whitman returned to Washington to work for the Department of the Interior's Indian Bureau, but soon returned home on Furlough to see George, who had been released from a Confederate prison camp.] He was still in Brooklyn eight days later, when Lee surrendered at Appomattox, and five days after that, when Lincoln was assassinated at Ford's Theatre in Washington. . . .

In May 1865 a new secretary of the interior, James Harlan of Iowa, was sworn in and immediately set out to clean up the department . . . and when he saw the copy of the 1860 *Leaves of Grass* that Whitman kept in his desk so that he could revise his poems during slow times at the office, he was appalled. On 20 June, Whitman, along with some other Department of the Interior employees, received a dismissal notice. . . . Whitman became a clerk in the attorney general's office the next day. He liked the work better—he aided in the preparation of requests for pardons from Confederates and later copied documents for delivery to the president and cabinet members—and held the job until he gave it up because of ill health in 1874. . . .

Taking a leave from his job, Whitman spent August and September 1866 in New York overseeing the printing of a new edition of *Leaves of Grass*. The book appeared near the end of the year, though the title page is dated 1867. It is the most carelessly printed and chaotic of all the editions. . . . He always believed that the history of *Leaves of Grass* paralleled his own history and that both histories embodied the history of America in the nineteenth century; thus, the 1867 edition can be read as his first tentative attempt to absorb the Civil War into his book. . . .

Whitman kept rearranging, pruning, and adding to *Leaves of Grass* to try to solve the structural problems of the 1867 edition. The book took a radically new shape when the fifth edition appeared; known as the 1871–1872 edition because of the varying dates on the title page, it was actually first printed in 1870. . . .

Democratic Vistas and *Passage to India*

In 1870 Whitman also published *Democratic Vistas* and *Passage to India*. . . . The title poem [of the latter] celebrates the work of engineers, especially the global linking accomplished by the transcontinental railroad, the Suez Canal, and the Atlantic cable. . . . For Whitman, modern material accomplishments were most important as means to better understanding of the "aged fierce enigmas" at the heart of spiritual questions. "Passage to India" is grand in conception and has had many admirers, but the rhetorical excesses of the poem—apparent in its heavy reliance on exclamation marks—reveal a poet not so much at odds with his subject matter as flagging in inspiration. . . .

If "Passage to India" and "After All Not to Create Only" were celebratory—perhaps at times naively so—*Democratic*

Vistas mounted sustained criticism of Reconstruction era failures. Based in part on essays that had appeared in *The Galaxy* in 1867 and 1868 *Democratic Vistas* responds to Thomas Carlyle's racist diatribe *Shooting Niagara: And After?* (1867), Carlyle's "Great Man" view of history made him impatient with democracy and opposed to efforts to expand the franchise in either the United States or England: the folly of giving the vote to blacks, he contends, is akin to that of going over Niagara Falls in a barrel. Whitman acknowledges the "appalling dangers of universal suffrage in the U.S." because of the "people's crudeness, vices, caprices"; he gazes piercingly at a society "canker'd crude, superstitious and rotten," in which the "depravity of our business classes . . . is not less than has been supposed, but infinitely greater." But, contrasting these current problems with "democracy's convictions" and "aspirations," he provides a ringing endorsement of democracy as intertwined with the fate of the United States—the two, in fact, are "convertible terms." Crucial to Whitman's program for strengthening democracy are what he calls "personalism"—a form of individualism—and the nurturance of an appropriate "New World literature." . . .

A series of blows turned 1873 into one of the worst years of Whitman's life. On 23 January he suffered a stroke; in February his sister-in-law Mattie, Jeff's wife, died of cancer; in May his mother's health began to fail. Partially paralyzed with weakness in his left leg and arm, Whitman arrived in Camden, New Jersey, three days before his mother's death on 23 May. He returned to Washington at the beginning of June, hoping to resume his job. But by the middle of the month he was back in Camden to stay, moving into a working-class neighborhood with his brother George and George's wife Lou. . . .

Whitman hoped that the [U.S.] Centennial Commission would ask him to write the national hymn, but five others were asked before Bayard Taylor accepted. Whitman celebrated the nation's centennial by bringing forth the variously labeled "Author's Edition" or "Centennial Edition" of *Leaves of Grass*. . . .

In 1881 a mainstream Boston publisher, James R. Osgood and Company, decided to bring out *Leaves of Grass* under its imprint. As had been the case more than twenty years earlier, when Thayer and Eldridge offered him respectable Boston publication, Whitman anticipated the benefits of high visibility, wide distribution, and institutional validation. Once again, however, things soon went awry. Oliver Stevens, the Boston district attorney, wrote to Osgood on 1 March 1882, "We are of the opinion that this book is such a book as brings it within the provisions of the Public Statutes respecting obscene literature and suggest the propriety of withdrawing the same from circulation and suppressing the editions thereof." The New England Society for the Suppression of Vice endorsed this view, and many reviews also predicted trouble for the book. . . . Osgood ceased selling *Leaves of Grass* and gave the [printing] plates to Whitman, who took them to the Philadelphia publisher Rees Welsh. Rees Welsh printed around six thousand copies of the book, and sales, initially at least, were brisk. . . .

Whitman had been living with his brother George; but when George retired and moved the family to a farm outside of town, Whitman refused to leave Camden. With what he had saved from the royalties from the 1881 edition of *Leaves of Grass*, combined with a loan from the publisher George W. Childs, he bought "a little old shanty of my own," and in March 1884 he moved into the only home he ever owned. . . .

Whitman continued writing, "garrulous," as he said, to the very end, but he worried that "Ungracious glooms, aches, lethargy, constipation, whimpering *ennui*, / May filter in my daily songs." The "Deathbed Edition" of *Leaves of Grass*, technically a republication of the 1881 edition with supplemental material, appeared in 1892. The first printing was bound in paper to make sure a copy reached the poet before his death. In this edition *Leaves of Grass* takes its final shape as authorized by the poet. . . .

Beset by an array of ailments, Whitman seemed to endure his final months through sheer force of will. . . .

He died on 26 March 1892. . . .

Whitman's Enduring Impact

Whitman's importance stems not only from his literary qualities but also from his standing as a prophet of liberty and revolution: he has served as a major icon for socialists and communists but has also been invoked occasionally by writers and politicians on the far right, including the National Socialists in Germany. Whitman's influence internationally has been most felt in liberal circles, where he is regarded as a writer who articulated the beauty, power, and always incompletely fulfilled promise of democracy.

"My book and the war are one," Whitman once said. He might have said as well that his book and the United States are one. Whitman has been of crucial importance to minority writers who have talked back to him—extending, refining, rewriting, battling, endorsing, and sometimes rejecting the work of a writer who strove so insistently to define national identity and to imagine an inclusive society. Critics sometimes decry Whitman's shortcomings and occasional failure to live up to his own finest ideals. But minority writers from Langston Hughes to June Jordan and Yusef Komunyakaa have, with rare exceptions, warmed to an outlook extraordinary for its sympathy, generosity, and capaciousness. Whitman's absorption by people from all walks of life justifies his bold claim of 1855 that "the proof of a poet is that his country absorbs him as affectionately as he has absorbed it." More than a century after his death, Whitman is a vital presence in American cultural memory. Television shows depict him. Musicians allude to him. Schools, bridges, truck stops, apartment complexes, parks, think tanks, summer camps, corporate centers, and shopping malls bear his name. One can look for him, just as he said one should, under one's boot-soles.

Whitman's Complexity Helps Readers Better Understand Democracy and Themselves

Richard Gambino

Richard Gambino is professor emeritus at Queens College, City University of New York. He is the author of books such as Blood of My Blood: The Dilemma of the Italian-Americans *and* Camerado, *a play about Walt Whitman.*

In the following viewpoint, Gambino examines Whitman's faith in the fundamental goodness of ordinary individuals regardless of race, gender, or sexual preference. While this faith is often explained as a by-product of Whitman's mysticism or naïveté, Gambino argues that it was Whitman's willingness to take an honest account of American democracy—its failures and successes alike—in works such as Democratic Vistas *(1871) that led him to conclude that his country's greatest assets were its common citizens rather than its intellectuals, politicians, or cultural elites. His appreciation for the average person was the framework for a vision of America as the home of unprecedented individual freedoms, and his revolutionary poetic style provided a striking example of such liberties applied to art. Even today, Gambino argues, Americans should follow in Whitman's footsteps and turn a critical eye toward the ideals and practices of their country while viewing fellow Americans as allies in the unending struggle for universal freedom.*

In 1848, 29-year-old Walt Whitman was for three months a reporter for the *Daily Crescent* in New Orleans, writing fluff pieces about local color and charm as seen through Yankee eyes. But he also saw darker spectacles there—streetside auctions of slaves—and six years later put his emotions into ironic verse:

Richard Gambino, "Walt Whitman," *The Nation*, vol. 277, no. 3, July 21/28, 2003, pp. 14–16. All rights reserved. Reproduced by permission.

I help the auctioneer, the sloven does not
half know his business . . .

Have you ever loved the body of a woman?

Have you ever loved the body of a man?

Do you not see that these are exactly the
same to all in all nations and

times all over the earth?

If any thing is sacred the human body is
sacred.

When he returned to New York, he became the editor of the
Brooklyn *Daily Freeman*, the nation's foremost voice of the
Free Soil movement, whose motto was, "Free soil, free labor,
free men!" He continued his advocacy of the movement, because of which, just before going to New Orleans, he had been
fired as editor of the *Brooklyn Daily Eagle*. But intimacy with
those in the movement had its effect. Whitman came to hate,
on the one side, the abolitionists for their fanaticism, most of
which went into infighting among themselves, and on the
other, the hypocritical and corrupt men of the Democratic
Party, all of them "born freedom sellers of the earth." He re-
signed from the *Freeman*, despondent. His faith rested in the
sympathy of the human heart, which had failed.

I have said that the soul is not more than
the body,

And I have said that the body is not more
than the soul,

And nothing, not God, is greater to one
than one's self is,

And whoever walks a furlong without sympathy walks to his own funeral

drest in his shroud.

Whitman's Faith Was Pragmatic

Whitman's faith in democracy flowed from the same source. It was not a faith resting on constitutionalism, legalisms, political science schemes, natural law or laws of history. It was rooted in a belief in the best of the human souls of ordinary citizens, often dismissed as his "mysticism." But when he was answering the challenge of whether the soul exists, his response did not depend on abstractions or esoterica but on the perceived experience of personal and historical growth. "No reasoning, no proof has establish'd it,/Undeniable growth has establish'd it." His faith in democracy rested on a distinctly American populism of pragmatic human experience. So in a twentieth century obsessed with ideological convictions that politics, and especially economics, determine human behavior and history, he was brushed aside as a quaint American naïf whistling in the dark.

Another common error is to take Whitman's faith in free humanity as a bombastic pollyannaism, or softheaded narcissistic, mystical messianism. Yes, he tells us that as a boy he was electrified by hearing a sermon by Elias Hicks of the Quaker Church on Joralemon Street in Brooklyn. (Hicks's faith in the human spirit was so radical that even his fellow Quakers denounced him as a heretic.) Whitman was captured by the idea that "the fountain of all ... truth ... [is] namely in *yourself* and your inherent relations," and that in this, Hicks was "a brook of clear and cool and ever-healthy, ever-living water." But young Whitman, who'd been pulled out of school at age 11, developed his own pragmatic, experiential populism, so would not become a Quaker. "Logic and sermons never convince,/ The damp of the night drives deeper into my soul." His mature populism was not of a Mary Sunshine kind.

Whitman's *Democratic Vistas* (1871) should be read by all Americans. It is a lengthy, scathing critique of American democracy's flaws at the time, and in ours—the flaws being the failings of its people and culture.

Photograph of an elderly Walt Whitman, taken in 1889. © Bettmann/Corbis.

I would alarm and caution ... against the prevailing delusion that the establishment of free political institutions, and plentiful intellectual smartness, with general good order, physical plenty, industry &c., (desirable and precious advantages as they all are,) do, of themselves, determine and yield to our experiment of democracy the fruitage of success. ...

I say we had best look our times and lands searchingly in the face.... The spectacle is appaling. We live in an atmosphere of hypocrisy throughout. The men believe not in the women, nor the women in the men. A scornful superciliousness rules in literature.... The great cities reek with respectable as much as non-respectable robbery and scoundrelism. In fashionable life, flippancy, tepid amours, weak infidelism, small aims, or no aims at all, only to kill time.

Populism and Free Verse

Whitman's enduring lesson about American democracy: "O I see flashing that this America is only you and me." No better, no worse. "The genius of the United States is not best or most in its executives or legislatures, nor in its ambassadors or authors or colleges or churches or parlors, nor even in its newspapers or inventors ... but always most in the common people."

Whitman's brand of populism mandated that he seek the liberation of people and culture, in a liberated poetic form. He did not invent free verse but embraced it and advanced it, against the ornamental, parade-ground regularities of meter and rhyme, which constrained his early poems to the point of banality.

Rhymes and rhymers pass away, poems
distill'd from poems pass away ...

America justifies itself, give it time, no dis-
guise can deceive it or conceal

from it, it is impassive enough.

In naturalism, freed from pie-in-the-sky otherworldliness:

And a mouse is miracle enough to stagger
sextillions of infidels.

In exquisite sensuality:

Out of the rolling ocean ... came a drop
gently to me,

whispering *I love you, before long I die,*

*I have travl'd a long way merely to look on
you to touch you.*

In sexuality:

Without shame the man I like knows and
avows the deliciousness of his sex,

Without shame the woman I like knows and
avows hers.

And in sexual orientation. Although he resisted admitting his homosexuality, even to absurdly claiming he had six illegitimate children, he did so to avoid, as with regard to all matters, being pigeonholed, and thus vulnerable to easy dismissal. But his "Calamus" poems are frankly homosexual, even celebratory in the sexual orientation (Calamus is a plant with a phalluslike head):

O here I last saw him that tenderly loves
me, and returns again never to separate
from me,

And this, O this shall henceforth be the token of comrades, this calamusroot shall,

Interchange it youths with each other! let
none render it back!

Whitman's sexual poems, like many others, were courageous. He was fired from a badly needed job as a clerk at the Interior Department in Washington by none less than the Secretary of the Interior himself. Secretary James Harlan stole Whitman's personal copy of *Leaves of Grass* from his desk, and noted, ironically, some of the heterosexual poems of the "Children of the Adam" section as "obscene."

The female form approaching, I pensive,
love-flesh tremulous aching . . .

The face, the limbs, the index from head to
foot, and what it arouses,

The mystic deliria, the madness amorous,
the utter abandonment.

Whitman's courage, and humor, extended to his last days. Wheelchair-bound, sleeping on a waterbed "like a ship or a duck" to relieve constant pain from multiple ailments, including bodywide TB [tuberculosis] and strokes, he described himself as "some hard-cased dilapidated grim ancient shellfish or time-bang'd conch (no legs, utterly non-locomotive) cast up high and dry on the shore-sands." (Years before, after suffering a stroke that left him paralyzed except for his head and one arm, he had brought himself back to complete mobility through his own efforts, including wrestling with saplings in woods.) He struggled against pain and paralysis to complete a ninth edition of *Leaves*. And succeeded.

Whitman Had Faith in America

Whitman saw in the risky experiment of a free people possibilities for a great polity, culture and morality. Three years before his death, in 1888, when he was 69, he wrote that there had been in his life one "purpose enclosing all, and over and beneath":

> Ever since what might be call'd thought, or the budding of thought, fairly began in my youthful mind, I had had a desire to attempt some worthy record of that entire faith and acceptance . . . which is the foundation of moral America.

His challenge to us, again typically American, is that the faith is to be fulfilled with each person and generation in the future.

Dear camerado! I confess I have urged you
onward with me,

and still urge you, without the least idea
what is our destination,

Or whether we shall be victorious, or utterly
quell'd and defeated.

Whitman's Love of Country Did Not Prevent Him from Speaking Out Against Injustice

David S. Reynolds

David S. Reynolds is professor of English and American studies at Baruch College and the Graduate Center of the City University of New York. His books include Walt Whitman's America: A Cultural Biography *and* John Brown, Abolitionist.

Throughout his life Whitman held complex, and often conflicted, opinions about the policies and practices of the United States and its people. He was a vehement supporter of the Union but despised government officials and their disregard for the poor and the downtrodden. He was sympathetic to social movements such as abolitionism and women's suffrage but leery of their tendency to disrupt and agitate social order. In the following viewpoint, Reynolds suggests that Whitman viewed his poetry as a vehicle for advocating a balance between the rights of the American individual—represented by the "I" persona featured in Leaves of Grass *(1855)—and the rights of Americans as a whole. Reynolds also states that Whitman viewed himself as a referee for the common citizen in the place of a president who was beholden to the interests of his mostly wealthy constituents.*

"Of all nations," Whitman wrote in 1855, "the United States . . . most need poets." America needed poets because, he believed, it failed to live up to its own ideals. It preached human equality but held more than three million African Americans in bondage. It stood for justice but treated the poor and the marginalized unjustly. It endorsed tolerance

David S. Reynolds, "Popular Culture, City Life, and Politics," in *Walt Whitman*. New York: Oxford University Press, 2005, pp. 24–40. All rights reserved. Reproduced by permission.

but discriminated against people of different ethnicities and religions. It was a democracy, but rampant corruption often negated the votes of the people.

There was a strong impulse in Whitman to lash out against America, for he saw himself as a literary agitator. He once declared, "I think agitation is the most important factor of all—the most deeply important. To stir, to question, to suspect, to examine, to denounce!" In the 1855 preface to *Leaves of Grass* he announced that in a morally slothful age the poet is best equipped to "make every word he speaks draw blood . . . he never stagnates."

Key lines in his poems echo this zestful tone: "I am he who walks the States with a barb'd tongue, questioning every one I meet"; "Let others praise eminent men and hold up peace, I hold up agitation and conflict."

Addressing Class Divisions and Political Corruption

He was responding to very real social problems. Class divisions were growing at an alarming rate. Whitman, whose family felt the constant pinch of poverty, lamented this economic inequality in his poetry. He could sound like Karl Marx or [American writer and social activist] George Lippard when he depicted the grotesque rich: "I see an aristocrat / I see a smoucher grabbing the good dishes exclusively to himself and grinning at the starvation of others as if it were funny, / I gaze on the greedy hog." In "Song of Myself" he repeated the charge often made by labor reformers that the "idle" rich cruelly appropriated the products of the hard-working poor:

Many sweating, ploughing, thrashing, and then the chaff for payment receiving,

A few idly owning, and they the wheat continually claiming.

The 1850s was also a decade of unprecedented political corruption, a time of vote-buying, wire-pulling, graft, and patronage on all levels of state and national government. There was historical reference, then, for Whitman's venomous diatribes, as in the 1855 preface where he impugned the "swarms of cringers, suckers, doughfaces, lice of politics, planners of sly involutions for their own preferment to city offices or state legislatures or the judiciary or congress or the presidency."

The chaos created by the slavery debate caused the collapse of the old party system. He wrote that the parties had become "empty flesh, putrid mouths, mumbling and squeaking the tones of these conventions, the politicians standing back in the shadow, telling lies." Those responsible for selecting America's leaders came "from political hearses, and from the coffins inside, and from the shrouds inside the coffins; from the tumors and abscesses of the land; from the skeletons and skulls in the vaults of the federal almshouses; from the running sores of the great cities."

Whitman's wrath against governmental authority figures extended to presidents. The administrations of Millard Fillmore, Franklin Pierce, and James Buchanan eroded his confidence in the executive office because of these leaders' compromises on the slavery issue. Whitman branded these three presidencies before Lincoln as "our topmost warning and shame," saying they illustrated "how the weakness and wickedness of rulers are just as eligible here in America under republican, as in Europe under dynastic influences." In "The Eighteenth Presidency!" he lambasted Pierce in scatological metaphors: "The President eats dirt and excrement for his daily meals, likes it, and tries to force it on The States. The cushions of the Presidency are nothing but filth and blood. The pavements of Congress are also bloody."

An Alternate America

Whitman was so critical of public figures that one might think that the final effect of his writing was bleak or negative. Quite the opposite, however, was true. It was precisely because of his disillusion with what America had become that he tried mightily to depict an alternative America in his poetry. *Leaves of Grass* was his democratic Utopia. It presented a transfigured America, one that *truly* lived up to its ideals of equality and justice. It was America viewed with an intense, willed optimism.

For all his severe words about his nation's shortcomings, Whitman did not join any of the radical reforms—Abolitionism, women's rights, working-class reform, the free love movement, and others—that were the main vehicles of social protest in his era. He had a conservative side. He loved to say: "Be radical, be radical, be radical—be not too damned radical." He once confessed, "I am somehow afraid of agitators, though I believe in agitation."

He feared what then was called "ultraism," or any form of extreme social activism that threatened to rip apart the social fabric. His ambivalence toward Abolitionism was especially revelatory.

On the one hand, he hated slavery and wished to see it abolished. During the 1840s he joined the so-called Barnburners, the antislavery wing of the Democratic Party. In his newspaper columns he vigorously protested against the proposed extension of slavery into western territories conquered during the Mexican War. In the 1848 election he worked for the Free-Soil Party, and in the early fifties his favorite politician was John P. Hale, the dynamic antislavery senator from New Hampshire.

Ambivalent About Abolitionism

At the same time, Whitman could not tolerate Abolitionism as it was advocated by the era's leading antislavery reformer, William Lloyd Garrison. He thought that Garrison went too far in his attacks on American institutions. Garrison condemned the Constitution as "a covenant with death and a compact with hell" because of its implicit support of slavery. His battle cry, "No union with slaveholders!" reflected his conviction that the North should immediately separate from the slaveholding South.

Whitman, who prized the Constitution and the Union, called the Abolitionists "foolish red-hot fanatics," an "angry-voiced and silly set." He hated the nullification doctrines of Southern fire-eaters as much as he did the disunionism of the Garrisonians. He explained, "Despising and condemning the dangerous and fanatical insanity of 'Abolitionism'—as impracticable as it is wild—the Brooklyn *Eagle* just as much condemns the other extreme from that."

His mixed feelings about the antislavery movement were also reflected in his middling position on the Fugitive Slave Law of 1850. On the one hand, he excoriated the law's supporters in his poems "Blood-Money," "Wounded in the House of Friends," and "A Boston Ballad."

At the same time, he believed that fugitive slaves must be returned to their owners. "MUST RUNAWAY SLAVES BE DE-LIVERED BACK?" he asked in "The Eighteenth Presidency!" His answer said it all: "They must. . . . By a section of the fourth article of the Federal Constitution." He called the Constitution "a perfect and entire thing, . . . the grandest piece of moral machinery ever constructed" whose "architects were some mighty prophets and gods." He valued the Constitution so highly that he was willing to support its directive that fugitives from labor must be returned.

His views were similar to Abraham Lincoln's, then a little-known Illinois lawyer and ex-congressman. Though morally opposed to slavery, Lincoln, like Whitman, hated Abolitionism because he put a high premium on the Union. He also supported the return of fugitive slaves because the Constitution demanded it.

Restoring Balance with Poetry

Fearing extremes, Whitman began tentatively testing out statements that balanced opposite views, as though rhetorical juxtaposition would dissolve social tensions.

His earliest jottings in his characteristic prose-like verse showed him attempting to balance antislavery and proslavery views in poetry. Fearing above all a separation of the Union, he penned lines in which an imagined "I" identified lovingly with both sides of the slavery divide:

I am the poet of slaves and of the masters
of slaves,[. . .]

I go with the slaves of the earth equally with
the masters

And I will stand between the masters and
the slaves.

Hoping to defend the Union while at the same time making room for the South's demand for states rights, he listed among "Principles We Fight For" the following:

The freedom, sovereignty, and independence
of the respective States.

The Union—a confederacy, compact, neither
a consolidation, nor a centralization.

When he wrote these words in 1846, he could not know that fifteen years later America itself would be divided between the Union, representing federal power, and the Confederacy, representing states rights. But he did see that the issue was one of momentous importance, at the absolute heart of American life. In a prose work he said that one of his main poetic objectives from the start was to solve "the problem of two sets of rights," those of "individual State prerogatives" and "the national identity power—the sovereign Union."

He shied away from movements that seemed to upset that delicate balance, and he tried mightily to restore that balance in his poetry. On this theme, the message of his poems was clear: balance and equipoise by poetic fiat. The poet was to be the balancer or equalizer of his land. "He is the arbiter of the diverse and he is the key," Whitman emphasized in the 1855 preface to *Leaves of Grass*. "He is the equalizer of his age and land . . . he supplies what wants supplying and checks what wants checking."

The People's Referee

Seeing that the Union was imperiled by Northern Abolitionists and Southern fire-eaters, in the 1855 preface he affirmed "the union always surrounded by blatherers and always calm and impregnable." The President would no longer be the people's referee; now the poet would be. The genius of the United States, he wrote, was not in presidents or legislatures but "always most in the common people," as it was better to be a poor free laborer or farmer than "a bound booby and rogue in office." His early poems are full of long catalogs of average people at work.

The basic problem of the conflicting rights of the individual and the mass was resolved imaginatively in the ringing opening lines of the first edition:

I celebrate myself,

And what I assume you shall assume,

For every atom belonging to me as good
belongs to you.

These lines radiated intense individualism and, simultaneously, intense democracy. The "I" celebrates himself but also announces his complete equality with others—the "you." Whitman announces to us that this individual-versus-mass tension can be resolved not by arguments over states rights and nationalism but by reference to something much larger: the physical operations of nature, "For every atom belonging to me as good belongs to you." All humans occupy the same physical world. They share atoms. There is a fundamental democracy in nature itself. Indeed, nature becomes a key unifying factor for Whitman. His title, *Leaves of Grass*, referred not only to the "leaves" (pages) of his volume but also to the earth's most basic form of vegetation—grass. Metaphorically, grass resolved the issue of individualism versus the mass. It was comprised of individual sprouts that could be admired on their own, as Whitman's persona does when he declares, "I lean and loafe at my ease observing a spear of summer grass." Also, grass was the earth's ultimate symbol of democracy and human togetherness, for it grew everywhere. As Whitman writes, "Sprouting alike in broad zones and narrow zones, / Growing among black folks as among white, / Kanuk, Tukahoe, Congressman, Cuff, I give them the same, I receive them the same."

Striking a Middle Ground

He knew that Southerners and Northerners were virtually at each others' throats, so he made a point in his poems constantly to link the opposing groups. He proclaimed himself "A Southerner soon as a Northerner, a planter nonchalant and hospitable down by the Oconee I live, / [. . .]At home on the hills of Vermont or in the woods of Maine, or the Texan ranch." When he addressed the issues of sectionalism and slavery in his poetry, he also struck a middle ground. In the 1855 preface he assures his readers that the American poet shall "not be for the eastern states more than the western or the northern states more than the southern." He writes of "slavery and the tremulous spreading hands to protect it, and the stern opposition to it which shall never cease till it ceases of the speaking of tongues and the moving of lips cease." The first half of this statement gently embraces the Southern view; the second half airs sharp antislavery anger but leaves open the possibility that it may be a very long time before slavery disappears.

Fearing the sectional controversies that threatened disunion, Whitman represented the Southern point of view in his poetry, as when he described a plantation: "There are the negroes at work in good health, the ground in all directions is cover'd with pine straw." At the same time, however, his view was close to that of antislavery activists of the 1850s who were emphasizing the humanity of African Americans. He takes a radically humanitarian view toward blacks several times in the 1855 edition. The opening poem, later titled "Song of Myself," contains a long passage in which the "I" takes an escaped slave into his house and washes and feeds him, keeping his rifle ready at the door to fend off possible pursuers. In another passage he actually becomes "the hounded slave," with dogs and men in bloody pursuit. In a third he admires a magnificent black driver, climbing up with him and driving alongside of him. "I Sing the Body Electric" presents a profoundly humanistic variation on the slave auction, as the "I" boasts how humanly valuable his slave is: "There swells and jets a heart, there all passions, desires, Teachings, aspirations, / [. . .]In him the start of populous states and rich republics."

Such passages help explain why his poetry has won favor among African American readers. The ex-slave and Abolitionist lecturer Sojourner Truth was rapturous in her praise of *Leaves of Grass.* The Harlem Renaissance writer Langston Hughes could talk of Whitman's "sympathy for Negro people," and June Jordan said, "I too am a descendant of Walt Whitman."

Deep Faith in Common People

Whitman's growing disillusion with authority figures sparked his deep faith in common people and in the power of populist poetry. America, he believed, desperately needed a poet to hold together a society that was on the verge of unraveling. He created his powerful, all-absorbing poetic "I" to heal a fragmented nation that, he hoped, would find in his poetry new possibilities for inspiration and togetherness. With almost messianic expectations for the impact of his writings, Walt

Whitman believed that America would reverse its downward course by seeing its diverse cultural and social materials reflected in the improving mirror of democratic poetry.

Democracy in Walt Whitman's Poetry

Whitman Forged His Own Theory of Democratic Poetics

Patrick Redding

Patrick Redding is an assistant professor of English at Manhattanville College in Purchase, New York.

Walt Whitman's idea of a new, democratic form of poetry—one accessible to everyday readers and free from traditional rules pertaining to rhyme, meter, and language—is intricately tied to his vision of an American republic that provides similar freedoms to its citizens. He often stressed, however, that his particular approach to poetry was only one of many possible ways of making the art form more democratic. Redding notes in the following viewpoint that poets and critics in the 1910s and 1920s formulated a theory of poetry that was less reliant on a "plain" style to distinguish it as democratic and was instead focused on the presentation of political ideas through a multitude of styles and voices.

"Has not the time arrived when, (if it must be plain said, for democratic America's sake, if for no other) there must imperatively come a readjustment of the whole theory and nature of Poetry?" As with so much else in his insistently proleptic [representing a future development as if it already existed] writings, Walt Whitman's urgent rhetorical question leaves the reader with little room for doubt. Here and elsewhere, Whitman aspires to be the foremost theorist of democratic poetics and at the same time its definitive practitioner. In other moments, however, Whitman will write in a more speculative vein, as if he were less sure what it meant to

Patrick Redding, "Whitman Unbound: Democracy and Poetic Form, 1912–1931," *New Literary History*, vol. 41, no. 3, 2010, pp. 669–90.

adjust the theory of poetry to the conditions of democracy. He writes more tentatively in his final preface to *Leaves of Grass* (1892): "I consider 'Leaves of Grass' and its theory experimental—as, in the deepest sense, I consider our American republic itself to be, with its theory." Writing within this retrospective frame of mind, Whitman implies that his theory of democratic poetry remains only one option out of a range of unspecified possibilities, making room for the rise of democratic bards in the future. In some moods, then, Whitman announces himself as an authoritative literary theorist, while at other moments he seems to realize that embracing democracy entails the evacuation of his own poetic authority: "He most honors my style who learns under it to destroy the teacher."

What is to be gained by uncoupling Whitman's theory of democratic poetics from the force of his poetic example? This essay attempts to answer this question by surveying some alternative accounts of democratic poetics. Without denying his seminal contribution to this general topic, I want to entertain the possibility of non-Whitmanian theories of democratic poetics, and in so doing, to point the way beyond *Leaves of Grass* as the normative standard for what it means to be "democratic" in poetry. Framing the issue as a theoretical problem serves to reverse the usual critical emphasis on Whitman's poetic "influence," which charts the galvanizing effect of his poetry upon such later figures as Carl Sandburg, Hart Crane, and Allen Ginsberg. Instead, this essay traces a specific moment in U.S. literary history, the decades of the 1910s and 1920s, in order to show how modernist critics applied Whitman's theory in ways that depart from his original ideas, or, in some cases, how these critics explicitly rejected his views. Whitman's uneven reception in these years highlights two surprising facts about U.S. literary history and its theoretical foundations: first, that alternatives to Whitman's theory of democratic poetics were already available in U.S. literary discourse as early as 1912; and second, that a strain of the literary movement known as modernism, often aligned in politics with fascism, authoritarianism, or aristocratic elitism, was actually quite preoccupied with forging a connection between poetry and political democracy. . . .

Whitman's Democratic Poetics

It will be useful to review the main tenets of Whitman's poetic theory. Generalizing from scattered comments made throughout his prose, Whitman's theory consists of three negative doctrines—the rejection of meter, the rejection of rhyme, and the rejection of conventional poetic diction—and one positive one, the use of the plain style. I am using "form" in the broadest sense to cover matters of rhythm and rhetoric. Needless to say, Whitman never described these four doctrines systematically, nor did he ever employ the phrase "democratic poetics." Yet for the past century and a half, literary critics from Edmund Dowden (1871) to Angus Fletcher (2004) have based their analysis of democracy and poetry on one of these doctrines, and cite Whitman as their authority for doing so.

Out of the four elements that compose his democratic poetics, Whitman is perhaps best known for associating democracy with the rejection of traditional poetic meter and rhyme: "The truest and greatest *Poetry*, (while subtly and necessarily always rhythmic, and distinguishable easily enough,) can never again, in the English language, be express'd in arbitrary and rhyming metre." Whitman's scorn for the laws of metrical measurement and rhyme, as we see in this passage from "Ventures, on an Old Theme" (1872), is linked directly to his sense of freedom from the "arbitrary" authority of monarchy and aristocracy. Whitman thus echoes the note on "The Verse" in *Paradise Lost*, where John Milton claims that "ancient liberty" has been "recover'd" from the "troublesome and modern bondage of Riming." In the "Preface to *Leaves of Grass*" (1855), Whitman extended this argument to include liberation from meter, too: rhyme and meter allow "abstract addresses" and "good precepts," he writes, but obstruct the autonomous expression of "the soul." "Perfect poems" follow a different logic from that used in traditional, rule-based forms: they illustrate "the free growth of metrical laws" and "take shapes as compact as the shapes of chestnuts and oranges and melons and pears, and shed the perfume impalpable to form." On this view, the absence of "rhyme and [metrical] uniformity" indicates a poet's commitment to the free expression of (human) nature. The democratic citizen was entitled to "free growth" in his private imagination just as in the public world of politics.

In addition to rejecting meter and rhyme, Whitman argued that the democratic poet must avoid artificial diction. He explains the third doctrine of democratic poetics in this passage from *Democratic Vistas* (1870): "To-day, doubtless, the infant genius of American poetic expression ... lies sleeping, aside, unrecking itself, in some western idiom, or native Michigan or Tennessee repartee, or stump-speech—or in Kentucky or Georgia, or the Carolinas—or in some slang or local song or allusion of the Manhattan, Boston, Philadelphia or Baltimore mechanic—or up in the Maine woods—or off in the hut of the California miner ..." American poetry becomes democratic only when it reproduces the vernacular idiom used in different regions of the nation. A poet who seeks out local dialects and conversational phrases proves his commitment to democracy by transgressing traditional class boundaries. By insisting on rugged, local speech, the democratic poet tears down the barrier between "the coteries, the art-writers, the talkers and critics" and working-class laborers like the "mechanic" or "miner."

Plain Style Embodies Democracy

Fourth, and finally, Whitman's commitment to democratic poetics sometimes takes the form of defending the plain style, as when he declares, "I will not have in my writing any elegance or effect or originality to hang in the way between me and the rest like curtains. . . . What I experience or portray shall go from my composition without a shred of my composition. You shall stand by my side and look in the mirror with me." In this appeal to artlessness, Whitman repeats a standard pastoral trope, one that reaches back to classical poets like Horace. Yet in Whitman's case, the plain style embodies the principles of equality and transparency that are emphatically linked to the ideals of modern democracy: "The messages of great poets to each man and woman are, Come to us on equal terms, Only then can you understand us, We are no better than you, What we enclose you enclose, What we enjoy you may enjoy." In addition to simplicity of style, then, Whitman's fourth doctrine of democratic poetics also aspires to immediate intelligibility, the kind of style that can appeal to a mass audience. In "Song of Myself," Whitman praises "words simple as grass, uncomb'd head, laughter, naivetè, / Slow-stepping feet, common features, common modes and emanations." Whitman idealized a mode of poetic speech that employed a low register of diction and a syntax that avoided hierarchical constructions like subordinate clauses. The "Preface to *Leaves of Grass*" famously employs a nonnormative style of punctuation, as if to record the movement of thought in real time, without the interference of formal systems of textural organization. Whitman's acceptance of what linguists call a "descriptive" rather than a "prescriptive" view of grammar means that he embraces ungrammatical phrasing in order to capture the way that people actually speak. Since all American poems partake of the ruffian spirit of the "great radical Republic," they will need to be delivered in a "loud, ill-pitch'd voice, utterly regardless whether the verb agrees with the nominative." Whitman believed that the plain style would enable the poet to represent the shared patterns of speech and understanding necessary to a thriving democratic public sphere.

American literary critics between 1912–1931 discussed all four of Whitman's doctrines, yet they did not necessarily find his doctrines logically consistent with one another, or even defensible on their own terms. Part of the problem is that Whitman's doctrines rely on multiple definitions of *form*, which lead his readers to talk about different things when discussing how poetry can represent democracy through its style. Sometimes these critics emphasize only one part of Whitman's theory (for example, his idea of the plain style) while ignoring a different aspect (for example, his view of meter). In other instances these critics will repudiate one of Whitman's central ideas—arguing, for example, that rhyme is actually more democratic than free verse because rhymed poetry is easier to memorize, and thus easier to pass along to younger generations and disparate social classes. Looked at individually, the critical approaches pursued by figures like Ezra Pound, Amy Lowell, Harriet Monroe, Josephine Preston Peabody, James Oppenheim, Max Eastman, Louis Untermeyer, James Weldon Johnson, Sterling Brown, Alain Locke, and Langston Hughes further confirm Whitman's authority as a theorist. Yet when these critics are viewed as a group, the variety of their responses serves to call Whitman's authority into question. As such, these modernist critics can teach us a surprising lesson about the politics of poetic theory. The lesson they collectively teach is that the "democratic" qualities of poetry need not reside primarily in the use of free verse, idiomatic language, plain style, or relationship to mass culture, but can be found in the development of political ideas within an individual career, or even across the stanzas of an individual poem. By the strength of their qualification and dissent, these critics help us to imagine what it might mean to speak of Marianne Moore, Wallace Stevens, John Ashbery, or Charles Bernstein as democratic poets *without* comparing their work to *Leaves of Grass*. Disenchanted with the results of an untenable political formalism, we might consider a more capacious formulation: that poems articulate democratic beliefs not just through a consistent facet of style, but also by reflecting the complex arguments, images, and shifts in tone and rhythm by which the voice of democracy declares itself on and off the page.

Whitman Celebrated the Creative, Risk-Taking Spirit of Capitalist Pioneers

Benjamin R. Barber

Benjamin R. Barber is a Distinguished Senior Fellow at Demos and Walt Whitman Professor of Political Science Emeritus at Rutgers University. He is the author of such books as Strong Democracy *(1984), the international best-seller* Jihad vs. McWorld *(1995), and* Consumed; How Markets Corrupt Children, Infantilize Adults, and Swallow Citizens Whole *(2007).*

In the following viewpoint, Barber maintains that each society's early capitalist history includes a number of colorful, rebellious, and sometimes roguish figures who took great risks and founded the fortunes from which future generations drew their wealth. Such adventurers are spiritual kin to Walt Whitman, who celebrated a robust, risk-taking ethos in "Song of the Open Road" and other works. Barber gives various examples of this type but points to one figure of particular interest in the context of Whitman: Whitman's contemporary William "Wild Bill" Rockefeller. Unlike his more famous son John D., the elder Rockefeller was a bombastic adventurer who exemplified Whitman's characterization of himself as "disorderly fleshy and sensual . . . eating drinking and breeding." According to Barber, this creative, swashbuckling type was essential to the foundations of not only American capitalism but also American democracy, which required an uprooting from earlier traditions in order to flourish. Although Whitman himself was more an adventurer of the imagination than an adventurer in actuality, his very personal, individualistic vision of democracy provides a theoretical context in which to understand these builders of American society.

Time and again, in each society's early capitalist history, roguish rebels emerge boasting the size of their appetites. "I inhale great draughts of space, / The east and the west are mine, and the north and the south are mine," proclaimed the swaggering Whitman in his "Song of the Open Road." Time and again they perceived their mission as holy when others saw it as profane. "I am larger, better than I thought, / I did not know I held so much goodness," exulted Whitman, adding the assurance "Whoever accepts me he or she shall be blessed and shall bless me."

It was Whitmanesque adventurers who helped open the trade routes, who made the contacts that led to exchange, repaired the road beds, laid the rails, mined the gold and silver, drilled for the oil on which others would found prudent fortunes. The first generation created first wealth or, at least, the conditions for creating first wealth, but they were not the accountants who accumulated it, counted it, and gave value to it and thus converted it into collective prosperity. These precapitalists were continental explorers like Lewis and Clark and their sea-faring predecessors who showed not just that there was a great, wide world beyond the safety of the hearth but how to tie it together through knowledge, communication, trade. They were wildcatters and miners in the United States who became small town founders, building saloons and general stores around Colorado silver mines and surrounding Pennsylvania oil rigs with opera houses and brothels. The towns came and went in the flash of a pyrite nugget in a prospector's hand and survived only as long as the oil kept pumping from a shallow field that might run dry in a year or a month. The little boomtowns mirrored the men who founded them. They came, flourished, acquired reputations beyond any substantial reality, then withered and vanished in the twenty years it took for the managers and accountants to bring the new wealth under control and rationalize it into a system of accumulation, distribution, and consumption which helped whole societies to prosper for centuries to come but which no longer needed the anarchic new towns and the outlaw adventurers who had built them.

In the modern American era there were still Whitmanesque figures such as Howard Hughes, larger than life personalities who multiplied, spent, lost, and regained fortunes. In Howard Hughes's case it was the fortune of his prudent father, of Hughes's Tool Company, and he squandered the money on a series of romantic escapades and entrepreneurial adventures involving aircraft, movies, women, real estate, Las Vegas hotels and casinos, and, of course, the aviation giant TWA. In all these fields he was a pioneer and speculator. He made his own laws. He led the way for more prudent followers, like Pan American Airways and the great Hollywood studios. Still more recently there are the pioneers of the electronic and digital revolution, Silicon Valley cowboys who made the imaginative leaps and took the risks in the 1960s and 70s and into the 80s, that allowed the consolidators and businessmen who established the monopolies and made the fortunes in the late 1980s and the 90s. These are not the Bill Gateses of the cyber-world, but people like William Gibson, John Perry Barlow (who wrote lyrics for the Grateful Dead), and the great cyber-pioneer Norbert Weiner—men with little respect for convention or tradition, or in some cases even for the law. Here again, it is the voice of Whitman we hear, talking about that mythical and magical American city:

Where the men and women think lightly of
the laws,

Where the slave ceases, and the master of
slaves ceases,

Where the populace rise at once against the
never-ending audacity of elected persons,

Where fierce men and women pour forth as
the sea to the whistle of death pours its
sweeping and unript waves,

. . .

Where the citizen is always the head and the
ideal, and President, Mayor, Governor and
what not, are agents for pay.

A Whitmanian Hero

There is, perhaps, no better American model of this Whitmanesque capitalist swashbuckler than the little known father
of a figure Americans know very well, John D. Rockefeller, the
iconic capitalist, founder of Standard Oil and calculating cre-
ator of cartel capitalism. If there is a contemporary of Whitman who embodies what is Whitmanesque in early capitalism,
then John D. Rockefeller's father William "Wild Bill" Rockefeller fits the bill. Ron Chernow, in his comprehensive and
engaging biography of John D. Rockefeller, spends several
chapters on the little known father. He describes the decade
after the Civil War as "the most fertile in American history for
schemers and dreamers, sharp-elbowed men, fast-talking swin-
dlers. A perfect mania for patents and inventions swept
America as everybody tinkered with some new contrivance. It
was a time of bombastic rhetoric and outsized dreams"—
bombastic rhetoric and outsized dreams to which Walt Whitman had already given a literary, a poetic voice. It was the ep-
och that Whitman both memorialized and incarnated within
himself. John D. Rockefeller—who was an accountant, keep in
mind, and initially an actuary, not a capitalist—naturally disdained his father's irresponsible ways, as well as all the dream-
dazed risk-takers like his father whom he met along the way
and whom he used and overcame on his way up fortune's lad-
der. Bill Rockefeller was one of the maddening mavericks, a
flimflam man and charming bigamist, raising two families,
counties apart, with more guile than sustenance; a character

63

also known as Devil Bill, who burnished his reputation as a gambler and a horse thief—not a camerado but a desperado. In fact, he was an actual snake oil salesman and had crafted schemes to sell all-purpose tonics and establish new businesses, one as hopeless as the next. Along the way, he made and lost several modest fortunes. He was a father who made early loans to his titan-to-be son, though obviously he never once grasped how much closer to the secrets of making money his son would become than he ever was.

Walt Whitman was not simply a literary alter ego to William Rockefeller but his actual contemporary. Rockefeller was Whitman's unwitting proxy, living out the character Whitman gave to himself when he wrote about those roughs—"Disorderly fleshy and sensual . . . eating drinking and breeding." He was a study in mobility, keeping two families and a host of businesses. But William's prudent son knew well enough that "the weak, immoral man was also destined to be a poor businessman," that as the frontiersman was only a moment in America's journey to maturation, the flimflam man was but a passing stage in the early life of capitalism—a man who created the conditions for capitalist accumulation but quickly came to stand between capitalism and its destiny, as Whitman, in a certain sense, stood between America's early history of the romantic roamer and its corporate destiny. Throughout his life John D. Rockefeller encountered and overcame men of the caliber his father had been. He had despised an early wildcatter partner named Jim Clark whom he called "an immoral man who gambles in oil," and he had bought him out with a bluff that was an early example of Rockefeller's own calculating risk-taking, which was always in the name of prudent management. He had disdained swaggering show-offs, like his first partner, who spent all he earned on fancy clothes and large watches to announce his wealth to an envious world he should have been diligently and quietly serving. He carried a like contempt for the boomtowns that must have fired his

Portrait of the American industrialist tycoon John D. Rockefeller (1839–1937), whose father, William "Wild Bill" Rockefeller, was a contemporary of Walt Whitman. Political theorist Benjamin R. Barber says Whitman and the elder Rockefeller were both the sort of adventurers whose dreams, albeit idealistic and foolhardy, were the seeds from which American democracy and capitalism grew. © Oscar White/Historical/Corbis.

father's imagination. Towns like Pithole Creek, where the first Pennsylvania oil wells had come in, represented to John D. the souls of men like his father writ large. They were cautionary fables, writes Chernow, of blasted hopes and counterfeit dreams, fables that renewed fears of the oil industry's short life span. Yet without William as ideology as well as biology there would have been no John D., no child of fortune, no fortune-founding capitalism either. John D. Rockefeller's success rested coldly on that earlier ethos cherished and memorialized by Walt Whitman that celebrated boundary-breaking creativity and narcissistic spontaneity, even though John D. knew the triumph of capitalism would await the suppression of this creative anarchy.

American Democracy's Unique Qualities

Bourgeois [middle-class] capitalism was able to root itself in firm soil only because of the deracination [uprooting] of those who came before. Deracination, it turns out, is a prime condition for democracy. Without an uprooting from feudal lands, without peasants turning away from the soil and looking up, there could be no new citizens, there could be no Renaissance, no Reformation, no trade, no capitalism. Perhaps most important of all, those early deracinated protocapitalist adventurers were, in fact, models for America's new democratic men—not European communitarians born of [English political philosopher Thomas] Hobbes and his anxieties about security against the war of all against all; not the Enlightenment empiricists for whom equality was but an entailment of common impulses and a common response to pleasure and pain; and not Virginia's farmers or the Carolina plantation owners whose ward government was a model of [Thomas] Jefferson's democratic aristocracy and who understood the relationship between liberty and private property (which did not exclude slavery). For these men were still rooted, still bounded by fences and property lines. They would become democratic in a European way, eventually overcoming the plantation system and its slavery and building free townships.

But that distinctively American democratic ethos associated with individualism and mobility was not nurtured in the soil or in some antediluvian state of nature but propelled by people on the move: cattlemen, woodsmen, searchers and pioneers, women and men who left the old thirteen colonies and settled the Tennessee territory that would give birth to Andrew Jackson, and then headed on west; those who set up artisan trades in St. Louis and Mason City and then pushed on, joining wagon trains on the way to California in search of gold.

New England township democracy was vital to American democracy—communitarian, rights based, representative, experienced, looking back to Europe. Yet the democracy of Whitman owes more to people like Roger Williams and Anne Hutchinson who fled the confines of Massachusetts. Whitman's democracy was robust, narcissistic, and innocent—unhinged and unpredictable. And it brought a new and quintessentially American egalitarianism. Not the equality of the social contract based on the abstract commensurability of beings with common natures, common needs, and common pleasures and pains but the concrete variety of actual people, each as worthy of respect as the next; not the equality of the state of nature, of all men *created* equal, but the *earned* equality of the teeming city, the equality of the trail, the equality of the wounded and dying, the equality that attaches to the dignity of all who live and die whether in female or male bodies, black or white, refined or rugged. Whitman's is the equality that comes after the fact of birth and with the fact of death, rather than the equality to which we are born—not the "right" but the actuality, incarnated in "Song of Myself" in Whitman's acknowledgment of the least of others as himself:

> The little plentiful manikins skipping
> around in collars and tail'd coats,
>
> I am aware who they are, (they are positively not worms or fleas,)
>
> I acknowledge the duplicates of myself, the
> weakest and shallowest is deathless with me,

What I do and say the same waits for them,

Every thought that flounders in me the
same flounders in them.

Whitman's Personal Democracy

The "kosmos" Walt Whitman discovered in his Manhattan self
was, in its deep individuality and infinite variety, always egalitarian. Right after he proclaimed those words "Unscrew the
locks from the door!" he wrote, "Whoever degrades another
degrades me ... and whatever is done or said returns at last
to me, /.../ I speak the password primeval ... I give the sign
of democracy, / By God! I will accept nothing which all cannot have." These seem less the words of a philosopher dream-
ing about egalitarianism than the oath of a trail boss, insisting
everyone in the wagon train will share their grub and their
grievances, what they think and what they experience; or the
words of a hospital nurse during wartime, measuring the
equality of death. (Whitman himself was of course a dreamer
of adventures rather than an adventurer himself, and his kin-
ship with these types was literary rather than actual.)

For the founders and for the political theorists from whom
they drew inspiration, equality was above all about politics,
about the right to equal access, one man one vote; because,
they believed, democracy was about elections and about the
accountability of those elected. Hence all the rights talk, the
Emancipation Proclamation and the Thirteenth, Fourteenth,
and Fifteenth amendments and then suffrage of women. In
this vision, equality was something to which people had a
natural right that had to be secured by constitutions and bills
of rights. Not for Walt Whitman. His democracy was about
how we live, how we experience and treat one another. Constitutional equality evokes uniformity (all are to be treated
alike) while Whitman celebrated variety. In "Song of Myself,"
he celebrated the self in everyone. It was an equality born of
experience rather than theory, of living among the many rather

than imagining their rights. Black Americans had won equality in theory through the words and proclamations that brought the Civil War to a conclusion. They have yet to fully experience what those words announced back then in the practice of American life today, except perhaps when they find themselves among those rough souls who measure their peers by spirit and energy and individuality. You are my equal not because it is your right (though it is) but because you *are* my equal. My individuality is yours, my thirst yours, my appetites yours, my differences yours. I am alike in my differences.

Whitman's sense of equality was the product of Comradeship: the sense of fraternity with which equality was affiliated in traditions less theoretical than that of the Social Contract [implied agreement between members of society], traditions in which, in Whitman's language, it was "amative [amorous]" and "adhesive" affection that drew people together, women and men, men and men, women and women—eros adumbrating [faintly indicating] the democratic republic: "It is by a fervent, accepted development of comradeship," Whitman writes in the *Preface* to the 1876 centennial edition of *Leaves of Grass* and "*Two Rivulets,*" "the beautiful and sane affection of man for man ... that the United States of the future ... are to be most effectually welded together, intercalated, anneal'd into a living union."

Whitman's Vision Today

It might of course be asked in this moment when the word "democracy" is on every tyrant's lips, in every conman politico's bag of tricks, in every hypocritical banker's vocabulary, whether Whitman's hardy democratic cameraderie and the distinctive notion of equality it evokes has any relevance. After all, it did and does little to confront the structural inequalities of capitalism (which helped breed the very individualism Whitman celebrates) or the failures of a more explicitly political democracy (about which it can perhaps be too self-absorbed and cavalier). As [Nobel Prize–winning author] J.M. Coetzee reminds us, Whitman himself recognized that the dismal proletarian uniformity and raw exploitation of the Gilded Age had little to do with the Jacksonian yeoman farmers and proud artisans he celebrated in "Song of Myself" and "A Song for Occupations." And though he supported the Civil War and emancipation, he was never an abolitionist nor a particularly ardent fan of the emancipated black man or of Reconstruction. Critics suggest that however agile and mobile his imagination might have been, Whitman was a loafer rather than a roamer.

Still, Whitman's equality feels real and palpable and speaks today to the endless variety of America, to its now global cities, teeming as ever with immigrants who are the hardy new specimens of an emerging global civil society—or not so civil society. For Whitman celebrates not government but society, and a pretty rough society at that: call it uncivil society. But like [French political scientist Alexis de] Tocqueville and [American philosopher John] Dewey, he understands, from the depth of his poetic intuition, that formal democracy depends on informal democracy, that voters must first be citizens. To be more than mere commands inscribed on paper, rights must be embedded in the habits and mores of a free people. In this sense it may be that Whitman's rough brief for uncivil society with all its abrasive edges, his equality of grittiness and sweat and sex and blood, is a firmer foundation for democracy than any written constitution on its own could ever be.

Whitman's "Song of Myself" Presents a Composite Democratic Individual

George Kateb

Political theorist George Kateb is the William Nelson Cromwell Professor of Politics Emeritus at Princeton University and the author of Patriotism and Other Mistakes *and* Human Dignity.

Although Walt Whitman sought throughout his career to champion universal rights and liberties as the foundation for democracy in the New World, he viewed the uniqueness of the individual—and the willingness to permit all others to be unique—as the most important building block of democratic culture. In the following selection, Kateb reads Whitman's "Song of Myself" as an example of this principle. Kateb highlights the apparent contradiction in the fact that the poem, which purportedly celebrates individualism as the highest ideal, also contains lines that seem to celebrate groups over individuals. Whitman reconciles this disparity by suggesting that every individual is in fact a unique composite of the same fundamental physical, psychological, and spiritual elements, and that by celebrating the individual we in fact celebrate society as a whole.

I think that Walt Whitman is a great philosopher of democracy. Indeed, he may be the greatest. As [American philosopher Henry David] Thoreau said, Whitman "is apparently the greatest democrat the world has ever seen." To put it more academically, he is perhaps the greatest philosopher of the culture of democracy. He writes the best phrases and sentences about democracy. By democratic culture, I mean these things especially. First, democratic culture is (or can be) the soil for the creation of new works of high art—great poems and moral writings, in particular. Second, democratic culture is (or is becoming) a particularist stylization of life—that is, a distinctive set of appearances, habits, rituals, dress, ceremonies, folk traditions, and historical memories. Third, democratic culture is (or can be) the soil for the emergence of great souls whose greatness consists in themselves being like works of art in the spirit of a new aristocracy. All these meanings are interconnected and appear in Whitman's writings throughout his life. Perhaps they receive their most powerful expression in "Democratic Vistas." But, in my judgment, the central meaning when we study Whitman is democratic culture as the setting in which what I have elsewhere called "democratic individuality" (a phrase close to Whitman's usage) is slowly being disclosed. I believe that the setting for democratic individuality is a greatly more powerful and original idea than any of the other ideas of democratic culture that I have just mentioned.

Democratic Individuality

In other places, I have tried to suggest that working together with [American author Ralph Waldo] Emerson and Thoreau, Whitman tries to draw out the fuller moral and existential significance of rights. These are the rights that individuals have as persons, and that the political system of democracy exists in order to protect, and also to embody in its workings. Democratic individuality is what rights-based individualism in a democracy could eventually become, once the political separation from the Old World was complete, and had already become, to some degree, in their time. I see the Emersonians as trying to encourage the tendency to democratic individuality, to urge it forward so that it may express itself ever more confidently and therefore more splendidly. In their conception of democratic individuality, I find three components: self-expression, resistance in behalf of others, and receptivity or responsiveness (being "hospitable") to others. My judgment is that for the Emersonians, the most important component of democratic individuality, by far, is receptivity or responsiveness. An individual's insistence on first being oneself expressively is valuable mostly as a preparation for receptivity or responsiveness: behavioral nonconformity loosens the hold of narrow or conventional methods of seeing and feeling (as well as preparing a person to take a principled stand in favor of those denied their rights).

This responsiveness or receptivity can also be described as a way—a profoundly democratic way—of being connected to others and to nature. As Whitman says in "Song of the Open Road": "Here the profound lesson of reception, nor preference nor denial." It is a way that deepens the sort of connectedness already present in rights-based individualism, but that only time and a steady commitment to rights can call forth. Time is needed because rights-based individualism is such a strange idea, and so untypical of past human experience, that those who live it and live by it—even though imperfectly—have to keep remembering, or keep learning as if they never knew, both the basic meaning and the further implications of what they profess and enact. And the steady commitment therefore turns out to be not so steady after all, but only as steady as the strangeness permits.

I would like to explore the connectedness that emanates from democratic individuality, as Whitman perceives and perfects it. He knows, let it be said immediately, the extent of the strangeness, and the steadiness for what it is, in democratic society. He says in the Preface, 1876, to *Leaves of Grass*: "For though perhaps the main points of all ages and nations are points of resemblance, and, even while granting evolution, are substantially the same, there are some vital things in which this Republic, as to its individualities, and as a compacted Nation, is to specially stand forth, and culminate modern humanity. And these are the very things it least morally and mentally knows—(though curiously enough, it is at the same time faithfully acting upon them.)"

In the Preface, 1872, he looks back on what he has been doing since he began writing *Leaves of Grass*. He says: "'Leaves of Grass,' already published, is, in its intentions, the song of a great composite *democratic individual*, male or female. And following on and amplifying the same purpose, I suppose I have in my mind to run through the chants of this volume, (if ever completed,) the thread-voice, more or less audible, of an aggregated, inseparable, unprecedented, vast, composite, electric *democratic nationality*." For me, Whitman's greatness does not lie in his pursuit of an image of a democratic American nationality, an image—in my phrase—of a particularist stylization of life. Such a notion strikes me as being of secondary importance at best. How important to the world is one more stylization? Even more, I do not think that the notion is consistent with the project of proposing "a great composite democratic individual." A "compacted Nation" (Preface 1876) is antithetical to a composite individual. Nationhood is too close to a conception of group identity: a shared pride in tribal attributes rather than in adherence to a distinctive and principled human self-conceptualization that may one day be available to persons everywhere in the world. As national poetry, "Drum-Taps" is full of a hateful belligerence: Whitman sees and exults in the indissociable bond between nationhood and war. No, Whitman's greatness lies in his effort, the greatest effort thus far made, to say—to sing—the democratic individual, especially as such an individual lives in receptivity or responsiveness, in a connectedness different from any other. Such connectedness is not the same as nationhood or group identity. (A later point in this essay is that it is not the same as "adhesiveness.")

"Song of Myself" Is the Key

I would like to suggest that his individualist effort attains its greatest height in the poem "Song of Myself." This is not to deny that everywhere in Whitman's work we will find resources for enriching or refining the poem's teaching. It is also true that he is sometimes less literal in this poem than he is elsewhere and later. But "Song of Myself" is of supreme value; it can organize one's reading of Whitman's body of writing. In thinking about this poem as the central work, one can make discoveries about the culture of democracy.

The poem is full of complexities. This democratic poem, like all of Whitman's best work, is immensely difficult; it is only barely accessible. His characterization of his own poems (in "As Consequent, etc.") perfectly suits "Song of Myself":

> O little shells, so curious-convolute, so
> limpid-cold and voiceless,
>
> . . . .
>
> . . . .
>
> Your tidings old, yet ever new and untrans-
> latable.

And if "Song of Myself" said—like any great work—unexpected things in its time, it remains—like any great work—altogether unexpected. So let us try to see what "Song of Myself" teaches. I mean to treat this poem as a work in political theory, which is what Whitman himself encourages (to say the least). Now and then, it is wise, however, to recall a line from "Myself and Mine": "reject those who would expound me, for I cannot expound myself."

Whitman makes major additions from version to version and omits a few lines here and there. We should be content, I think, with the last version, that of 1891–92, even though it is interesting to study Whitman's changes. One change, however, should be noticed. Whitman did not call the poem "Song of

Myself" until 1881. In the first version of 1855, the poem, like all the poems in the first edition of *Leaves of Grass*, had no title. Thereafter, the poem is successively called "Poem of Walt Whitman," "Walt Whitman," and finally, "Song of Myself."

All of its various titles are odd—as, indeed, the title of the collection (*Leaves of Grass*) is odd. The poem's titles are odd because when we read it, we do not find the poem autobiographical, except in a few unimportant details. The egotistical titles are not the titles of an egotistical work. Nor is the work self-referring or self-revelatory in any usual sense. There is scarcely anything intimate in it. It tells no story about the writer. Perhaps it would be all the more odd if the poem were self-revealing: Until rather late in life, Whitman had little fame. Why should anyone have cared to hear an account of his life in 1855?

Individuals' Infinite Potentialities

In the very first section of the poem, Whitman says:

> what I assume you shall assume,
>
> For every atom belonging to me as good
> belongs to you.

Notice the extreme rapidity of movement in mood in these two lines. "What I assume you shall assume" seems to indicate that the poet is demanding that his readers obey him in their thought: a sentiment worse than egotistical. But then, in the next line, he is telling us that the reason we are to assume what he assumes is that "every atom belonging to me as good belongs to you." It is not that we must obey him as we read him. Rather, if we understand the poem, we will see that the poet and his readers are alike, and therefore we will come to assume what the poet does. In telling of himself, the poet is telling us about ourselves: That is what is to be assumed. His words about himself are words about us. As he proclaims in the climax of one of his long and observant catalogs of expressive human roles and functions: "of these one and all I weave the song of myself" (sec. 15). In a Notebook entry (1855–56), Whitman says: "I have all lives, all effects, all hidden invisibly in myself. . . . [T]hey proceed from me." In fact, if luck had made any of his readers democratic poets (and contingency is the thing that makes the greatest difference), we would have said or sung poems with the same purport as "Song of Myself":

> (It is you talking just as much as myself, I
> act as the tongue of you,
>
> Tied in your mouth, in mine it begins to be
> loosen'd.) (sec. 47)

We are alike in a certain way: Living in a rights-based democracy enables and encourages a certain recognition of likeness. What is the nature of this likeness? Whitman says that "every atom belonging to me as good belongs to you." Let us emphasize the word "atom." What does it mean in this poem? An atom is a potentiality, I think. Every individual is composed of potentialities. Therefore, when I perceive or take in other human beings as they lead their lives or play their parts, I am only encountering external actualizations of some of the countless number of potentialities in me, in my soul. These atoms are in everyone; hence "every atom belonging to me as good belongs to you." The difficult and important complication is that in one's experience of others, one encounters their personalities, not their souls. The world contains an amazing diversity of personalities. Contingency has a great share in realizing any potentiality. Souls, however, are the same: infinite potentialities. . . .

An Understanding of Equal Rights

In any case, Whitman is suggesting two main things. All the personalities that I encounter, I already am: That is to say, I could become or could have become something like what others are; that necessarily means, in turn, that all of us are always indefinitely more than we actually are. I am potentially all personalities, and we equally are infinite potentialities. Whitman's poetic aim is to talk or sing his readers into accepting this highest truth about human beings. Democracy covers it over less than all other cultures. If people take thought, they will have to acknowledge that, first, they have all the impulses or inclinations or desires (for good and for bad) that they see realized around them, even if they act on other ones, and consequently, second, that each of us is, in Emerson's word, an "infinitude," or, in another formulation of Emerson's, "an inner ocean." The deepest moral and existential meaning of equal rights is this kind of equal recognition granted by every individual to every individual. Democratic connectedness is mutual acceptance. Rejection of any other human being, for one reason or another, for apparently good reasons as well as for bad ones, is self-rejection. A principal burden of Whitman's teaching, therefore, is that the differences between individuals do not go as deep as the commonalities. Personality is not the (secular) soul. He explicitly says in "To You" that every endowment (talent) and virtue is latent in every individual, not merely every impulse or desire.

If I am right in the suggestions that I am making concerning the poetic aim of "Song of Myself," the result is rather strange (to use that word again). The great poem of individualism in a democracy is not individualist in any conventional sense. After all, to be individual originally meant to be indivisible. Clearly, "Song of Myself" is not asking us to pretend that we are indivisible. It is more than a matter of having aspects: soul, body, self, and personality. The (secular) soul itself is a crowded house. (Later on, in "One's-Self I Sing" [1867], he can refer to each of us as "a simple separate person." If he is still consistent with his earlier teachings, "simple" would have to connote unpretentious, yet precious, but not indivisible.) I read the odd and funny line, "It is time to explain myself—let us stand up" as a pleased reference to inner multiplicity (sec. 44). More famously, he says toward the end of the poem:

Do I contradict myself?

Very well then I contradict myself,

(I am large, I contain multitudes.) (sec. 51)

Our potentialities are not only numberless but—and for that reason—conflicting. We are inhabited by tumultuous atoms. We are composite, not even composed. In "Crossing Brooklyn Ferry," he goes so far as to posit "myself disintegrated, everyone disintegrated." I think that Whitman would have admired [philosopher Friedrich] Nietzsche's convolutedly Platonic saying that the body is "but a social structure composed of many souls." Whitman's radicalism shows in his distance from Plato's dream of harmony among the aspects of the individual and of stillness in the house of the potentialities.

Yet, in abandoning in "Song of Myself" the idea that the individual is indivisible, he is not creating an altogether new sense of individualism. He sees that more than a few American individuals are aware of their own composite nature and of their own undefinability. The telling point is not so much that the United States is a pluralist society made up of all psychological and sociological types as it is that democratic individuals see (if only unsteadily) that each of them contains the raw material of all types, yet is more than any type or all types, and is even more than its special personality. (Of course, it counts for a good deal that the democracy is as expressively diverse as it is, and is so on a plane of equality rather than hierarchically.)

Let me now summarize provisionally what Whitman is doing in "Song of Myself." He is presenting a portrait of himself, but it is not a portrait of his social or everyday personality. It is not a story, either, of the things that he has done or the particular experiences that have shaped his personality or even shaped the course of his life. To tell these things is not to tell of what is most important about himself. "Song of Myself" is not like a photo or realistic drawing; but it is, nevertheless, the best and fullest account of himself—and, also, of course, of everyone else.

Whitman's Principle of Democratic Comradeship Rested on Bonds of Love Between Men

Stephen Alexander

Stephen Alexander holds a doctoral degree in modern European philosophy and literature from the University of Warwick, where he wrote his dissertation on D.H. Lawrence.

In the following selection, Alexander uses the essay "Democracy" by British writer D.H. Lawrence, in which Lawrence rejects Walt Whitman's idealistic notions of the equality of individuals and the overarching unity of all beings in the universe, as a starting point for an investigation into the one element of Whitman's idealism that Lawrence agreed with: homosexual love as a conduit for a new set of societal values based on the liberty of the individual. Alexander points to Whitman's experiences with male soldiers during the Civil War as the impetus for this idea and cites a passage in Democratic Vistas *(1871) as an illuminating example of Whitman's fusion of democracy with desire.*

In 1919, [British novelist D.H.] Lawrence produced an important essay entitled 'Democracy', which grew out of his writings on [Walt] Whitman for the book that would eventually be published in 1923 as *Studies in Classic American Literature.* Each of the four parts of the above essay uses Whitman as its starting point, which suggests that, for Lawrence, democracy was inconceivable without reference to the 'good gray poet' and it illustrates how Lawrence, like Whitman, under-

Stephen Alexander, "Whitman and Lawrence: Towards a Democracy of Touch," *PN Review*, vol. 34, no. 3, January/February 2008, pp. 31–34. All rights reserved. Reproduced by permission.

stands the political as a field of theory and action in which the writer plays an important role. What is perhaps most interesting about this essay is, as Michael Herbert points out, the fact that it recalls some of Lawrence's earlier revolutionary demands for the abolition of the private ownership of land, industry and commerce. Lawrence writes, for example: 'If we are to keep our backs unbroken, we must deposit all property on the ground, and learn to walk without it. We must stand aside. And when many men stand aside, they stand in a new world . . . This is the Democracy, the new order. In this manner, Lawrence also anticipates his later political thinking developed in the *Lady Chatterley* writings; particularly his Whitmanesque notion of a 'democracy of touch' founded upon what he calls 'phallic consciousness' or, simply, 'tenderness'. I'll say more about this idea shortly, but, prior to this, I'd like to make a few further comments on the 'Democracy' essay.

A Rejection of Whitmanian Democracy

What interests me about this work, other than Lawrence's desire to address the property question, is the fact that it explicitly rejects the two laws or principles for the establishment of democracy put forward by Whitman: namely, the Law of the Average and the Principle of Identity.

It is obvious that the first of these laws involves a process of crude reductionism in which the flesh and blood individual is conveniently replaced by a mathematical unit. Lawrence points out how our fetishisation of the Average Person has resulted in what was once a strictly theological concept (the equality of all souls before God) becoming a political ideal (the equality of all citizens before the State) upon which rests 'all the vague dissertations' concerning human rights and the social perfectibility of Man.

Whilst conceding that the Average Person does represent what all men and women may need 'physically, functionally, materially and socially', Lawrence is adamant that there is no genuine equality 'save by the arbitrary determination of some ridiculous human Ideal'. Further, whilst he is happy to see the basic needs of all people living together within society met (that is to say, the social provision of food, clothing, housing etc. according to common necessity as determined by the Law of the Average), he insists that everything outside or beyond material need and common necessity depends on the individual man or woman and that he or she should be left alone accordingly to freely develop their own uniqueness and determine their own status within what [German philosopher Friedrich] Nietzsche would call an 'order of rank' (*Rangordnung*).

For Lawrence, then, the modern state exists only to guarantee the basic material means of existence: nothing more. It has no vital meaning or purpose beyond this and our political leaders should be regarded as no more than functionaries. The last vestiges of 'ideal drapery' should be stripped away from the State and from politics. For Lawrence, a kind of tolerant contempt for those in government is a sign of social evolution and political maturity. Not only is it absurd to think of politics in ideal terms but, Lawrence argues, it is ultimately genocidal too; for only ideal concerns wage war 'and slaughter indiscriminately with a feeling of exalted righteousness.

As for Whitman's second principle of One Identity, Lawrence pooh-poohs this as yet another form of fatal idealism. Or, rather more precisely, as a return of the old dogma of monotheism in which all things are held to be an emanation of the Supreme Being, or God, who, it turns out upon closer inspection, is simply the Average Person writ large: 'But instead of a magnified average-function-unit, we have here the magnified unit of Consciousness or Spirit.'

It's all very nice theoretically to inflate our own consciousness to infinity and cosmic oneness á la Whitman, but, once more, it ultimately ends tragically as we realise with increasing nihilism following the death of God, that we remain mortal, limited, and alone. Lawrence feels it is vital that we learn how to be content within our own skins: 'Better, far better', he writes, 'to be oneself, than to be any bursting Infinite, or swollen One-Identity'. Lawrence's democracy of touch, as we will see, is based precisely on this teaching of limited singularity—not on any notion of merging into oneness with others, which is 'a horrible nullification of true identity and being' and results in the political movements that have brutally characterised modernity (from imperialism to republicanism; from communism to fascism).

Whitman's Eroticisation of Democracy

Lawrence, then, for all his admiration, is often overtly hostile to Whitman and the latter's notion of democracy. Not only does he flatly refuse to worship the Average, but so too does he reject Oneness and Whitman's love of Personality: 'Never', declares Lawrence rather magnificently, 'trust for one moment any individual who has unmistakable personality. He is sure to be a life-traitor.' But what Lawrence does seem to find irresistible in Whitman is the latter's flooding of the political with desire and I'd like now to turn to an earlier version of the Whitman study, also written in 1919, in which Lawrence explicitly addresses and develops the poet's perverse eroticisation of democratic political theory via his concept of manly love.

If this essay tells us something vital about Whitman's work, so too does it tell us something important about Lawrence's own intensely ambivalent position on homosexual desire and the significance he gives to anal sex in particular as a method for attempting what Nietzsche would term a 'revaluation of all values' (*Umwerthung alter Werthe*).

As in later versions of the study, Lawrence argues that Whitman, having failed in his attempt to dissolve himself into universal, democratic oneness via the love of Woman, is obliged to turn elsewhere for the establishment of a vital circuit of polarisation; namely, to the manly love of comrades.

This Civil War photograph depicts Armory Square Hospital in Washington, DC, which Walt Whitman regularly visited to cheer wounded soldiers. © Medford Historical Society Collection/Corbis.

The male need for initiation into some kind of homo-erotic mystery religion was, according to Lawrence, something well known to ancient esoteric priesthoods 'thousands of years before Plato', but Whitman was the first modern to reaffirm this truth 'from sheer empiric necessity', having discovered that 'the last stages of merging were impossible between things so categorically different as man and woman'.

Whitman, as we know, was struck and seduced by the intense comradeship of the front-line soldiers during the American Civil War and it was around this time he began to infuse the idea of democracy with desire. In a prose text entitled *Democratic Vistas*, Whitman discriminates between *amative* (i.e, what we would now term heterosexual) and *adhesive* (i.e. homosexual) love, privileging the latter as crucial to the formation of a new, wider type of democratic community in contrast to the prevailing liberal-bourgeois model. In a rather touching and radical passage worth quoting at length he writes:

> It is to the development, identification, and general prevalence of that fervid comradeship (the adhesive love, at least rivalling the amative love hitherto possessing imaginative literature, if not going beyond it), that I look for the counterbalance and offset of our materialistic and vulgar American democracy, and for the spiritualization thereof. Many will say it is a dream and will not follow my inferences: but I confidently expect a time when there will be seen ... manly friendship, fond and loving, pure and sweet, strong and lifelong, carried to degrees hitherto unknown, not only giving tone to individual character and making it unprecedentedly emotional, muscular, heroic and refined, but having the deepest relation to general politics. I say democracy infers such loving comradeship ... without which it will be incomplete, in vain and incapable of perpetuating itself.

Whitman then goes on to add that *Leaves of Grass* was specifically composed in order to arouse 'endless streams of living, pulsating, terrible, irrepressible yearning' and indicates how the 'Calamus' poems in particular are full of political significance, invoking as they do the democracy to come founded upon 'the beautiful and sane affection of man for man'. Lawrence, who describes this manly love of comrades as Whitman's most 'wistful' theme, never quite accepts this; rather, he maintains that it is heterosexual coition which results in the 'perfect life-current' upon which all human being rests. Because of this, his democracy of touch is ultimately established between men and women and is not an exclusively all-male arrangement.

Whitman Was Not Socially—or Sexually—Isolated, and This Informed His Vision of Democratic Community

Michael Moon

Michael Moon is a professor at Emory University, specializing in American literature and culture, and the author of Disseminating Whitman: Revision and Corporeality in "Leaves of Grass."

For scholars of Walt Whitman's work, the conflict between the poet's twin personas as celebrator of the masses and champion of individualism is a perplexing problem. In the following viewpoint, Moon opposes those modern critics who envision the real Whitman—rather than his literary persona—as an isolated and even cantankerous man whose poems of spiritual and sexual union with others were simply the fantasies of a lonely writer. Pointing to the criticism of Whitman's contemporaries and to the lists of names that the poet kept in his notebooks, Moon argues that Whitman's active engagement with the people around him led to the radical change in his poetic style in the 1850s and to his increasing insistence that every individual represents a universe of goodness.

Walt Whitman projects two equally powerful, in some ways quite contradictory, versions of himself through his poetry. I believe we are to take this contradictoriness as part of the design of the writing, this being the poet who famously indemnified himself at the beginning of his career by

Michael Moon, "Solitude, Singularity, Seriality: Whitman Vis-à-vis Fourier," *ELH: English Literary History*, vol. 73, no. 2, Summer 2006, pp. 303–23. All rights reserved. Reproduced by permission.

announcing, "Do I contradict myself? Very well then, I contradict myself; / I am large, I contain multitudes." One of these versions of himself is as the celebrator of the American social mass, in which he is part of and in the midst of the throngs of the citizens, laborers, loafers, and holiday-makers the poetry evokes: "I Hear America Singing." The other is the "Solitary Singer," the title of Gay Wilson Allen's long-standard 1955 biography of Whitman, a designation for the poet that derives from his own writing, as in the line, "Solitary, singing in the West, I strike up for a New World," from "Starting from Paumanok" (line 13), or the "singer solitary" he styles himself at the dramatic climax of another 1860 poem, "Out of the Cradle Endlessly Rocking" (line 150).

Whitman as an Isolated Figure

Many of Whitman's most influential critics have emphasized the singular and supposedly isolated figure who inhabits some of the poetry, almost to the exclusion of the merging and massifying self and body that impel so much of the rest of it. Allen, Edwin Haviland Miller, Quentin Anderson, and Paul Zweig, for example, have, for all their considerable differences, tended to privilege a version of Whitman as a figure of lonely pathos. To this way of thinking, such self-figurations of Whitman's in his poetry as the hyperactively amorous speaker in yet another 1860 poem ("So Long!") who presents himself as leaping off the pages of *Leaves of Grass* into the arms of his readers (line 57), or the speaker who claims in "Song of Myself" to "fly the flight of the fluid and swallowing soul" (section 33, line 800), are simply the pitiful fantasies of a morbidly withdrawn man, about an exuberant manner of living of which he could only dream.

This version of Whitman as a person isolated by his remarkable gifts and anguished by some irresolvable sexual secret or ambiguity was solidly in place by 1955, the year of the centennial celebrations of the publication of the first *Leaves of*

Grass and of the appearance of Allen's biography. The satura-
tion of such an image with two such familiar shibboleths [dis-
tinguishing beliefs] of the 1950s as the open secret of the
closet and the supposedly terrible price of artistic genius makes
it instantly recognizable as a piece of Cold War cultural ideology. The dominance of these motifs in Whitman criticism and
biography from the 1950s through the 1970s represented a
long-lasting foreclosure of another, quite different paradigm—
one that had been established during the poet's lifetime
through the work of such critics as the Anglo-Irish man of
letters Edward Dowden. In 1871 the young Dowden published
in the *Westminster Review* one of the first strong essays to insist that what is distinctive about Whitman's poetry is a product of the intensity of his interest in what Dowden calls "men
of every class," and his poetry's relative lack of interest in any
single or particular individual, himself included—despite the
commonly-made mistake of reading "Song of Myself" as a
paean to narcissism, Whitman's in particular. Dowden argues:

> No single person is the subject of Whitman's song, or can
> be; [for him,] the individual suggests a group, and the group
> a multitude, each unit of which is as interesting as every
> other unit, and possesses equal claims to recognition. Hence
> the recurring tendency of his poems to become catalogues
> of persons and things. . . . Men and women are seen en
> masse. . . . Whitman will not have the people appear in his
> poems by representatives or delegates; the people itself, in its
> undiminished totality, marches through his poems, making
> its greatness and vitality felt.

Whitman's Lists

Much gay criticism on Whitman since Robert K. Martin's pio-
neering book of 1979 has been instrumental in disrupting the
critical consensus that had held for much of the twentieth
century about his alleged solitariness and anomalousness as
person and poet. The reinvigoration of the long-established,
but temporarily disrupted, practice of reading Whitman as a

Walt Whitman with an intimate friend, Peter Doyle. © Historical/Corbis.

fascinated and ardent member of groups and masses of men has had the effect of producing two quite different ways of responding to much of his writing. If reading the lists of names of hundreds of men and boys whom Whitman encountered in his daily rounds in Brooklyn and Manhattan and with which he filled the pages of some of his 1850s notebooks brings tears to the eyes of Whitman biographer Paul Zweig, who imagines the poet more or less stuck in a state of wistful, unavowable desire for these men, critic Charley Shively, in his account of these same lists, assumes that Whitman got down with every last man and boy he names; for Shively, only the readily decodable symbols are missing that would inform us whether the tricks catalogued in this little black book were oral, anal, or manual; active or passive; a two-way, a three-way, a small circus, or whatever.

Why did Whitman in the 1850s make long lists—of the names of men, often young men, with frequent brief annotations about their ages, their occupations, their appearances, and where he had encountered them: "Wm Culver, boy in bath, aged 18 (gone to California 1856)"; "Sam, young fellow I met at Dominick Colgan's [the] plumber"; "Mark Ward—young fellow on [F]ort Greene—talk from 10 to 12, / John Sweeten—tall, well-tann'd, born in New Jersey,—driver"; "Aaron B. Cohn... appears to be 19 years old—fresh and affectionate young man—spoke much of [another] young man named Gilbert L. Bill (of Lyme, Connecticut) who thought deeply about *Leaves of Grass*, and wished to see me"; "Charley (black hair and eyes—round face) 4th av."; "John Kiernan (loafer young saucy . . . pretty good looking)"?

Without assuming that such lists are simply the names of Whitman's tricks, we can, I believe, draw from them a sense of the radically enlarged social, political, and erotic possibility that began to impel his writing in the mid-1850s. It has long been a commonplace in Whitman criticism to speculate about what the elusive quantity x was that allegedly transformed the very ordinary-seeming writer that Whitman had been into the visionary poet he suddenly became in his mid-thirties. Was it reading [Ralph Waldo] Emerson's essays, being told that he was a genius by a phrenologist reading the bumps on his head, or the volatile political atmosphere of New York City in the years leading up to the outbreak of the Civil War? Each of these three factors has been put forward at different times as the likely precipitant of Whitman's transformation into a powerful poet. Or was it Whitman's belated discovery, sometime in his early thirties, of masturbation? (Jerome Loving proposes this last possibility in the most recent full-scale biography of the poet.)

Whitman's Transformation

I don't myself believe that there can be any single explanation of what catalyzed Whitman's transformation. For me, the Whitman who wrote the poetry of the first four editions of *Leaves of Grass* between 1855 and 1867 had everything in common, so to speak, with the person who had been involving himself in the increasingly hectic life of New York City for fifteen or twenty years before he started writing remarkable poetry. Part of what I want to retain for my purposes here from the keen insights of such early liberal-democratic critics of Whitman as Dowden is the possibility that it was a powerful set of discoveries about the immense worthiness, lovability, and desirability of ordinary men, and of one ordinary man for another, that began to electrify Whitman's previously rather pedestrian poetry. What much of Whitman's poetry of the mid-to-late 1850s announces and avers, I believe, is that every one of the men he names on the long lists in his notebooks potentially constitutes in himself and for his "camerados" an entire world of intense goodness and pleasure: a whole "cosmos"—to use a favorite term of Whitman's and of his age—instinct with love and joy. So does every other person, but this list-maker is especially cued into the young men he names because each of them carries some kind of erotic charge—actual or potential—for him, and he, actually or potentially, for each of them.

Dowden speaks, in the passage I have quoted, of "the recurring tendency of [Whitman's] poems to become catalogues of persons and things," and these so-called catalogs have been one of the most frequently discussed topics in, and one of the most widely parodied features of, Whitman's poetry. The "tendency" to catalog actually "recur[s]" notably only in his poetry of the 1850s, as, for example, in sections 15 and 33 of "Song of Myself," "Crossing Brooklyn Ferry," "By Blue Ontario's Shore," "Salut au Monde!," or "A Song for Occupations." I would relate this cataloging habit of Whitman's early poetry to the long lists of men's names he made in notebooks during the same years, in order to argue that these practices bespeak an epistemology—not of the closet, of the kind Eve Kosofsky Sedgwick has anatomized so brilliantly, but of "the street or ferry-boat or public assembly," as Whitman puts it in "Crossing Brooklyn Ferry"—an epistemology of any space in the city where the poet might wedge himself into throngs of young men and, as he writes, "f[eel] their arms on my neck as I stood, or the negligent leaning of their flesh against me as I sat" ("Crossing Brooklyn Ferry," section 6, lines 81, 80). Finding himself squeezed between some other male bodies and at the same time propping up or supporting the weight of yet other male bodies enables the poet to know or learn crucial things about himself and his world and the others who constitute it which he could learn by no other means that he can envision. Perhaps rather than simply discovering masturbation or homosexuality, Whitman began to realize or to imagine sometime around the mid-1850s that some kinds of social and political contexts and public supports were beginning to emerge for this surprising and transformative new kind of knowledge or understanding he had recently discovered among the throngs of young men in Brooklyn and Manhattan. What I imagine Whitman possibly recognizing at this point is that erotic desires and activities between and among men were just beginning to become the subject of public discourses in which they might conceivably come to be understood by increasingly larger numbers of people as constituting potentially world-making, life-affirming practices, rather than the so-called filthy abominations they had widely been considered to be. Whitman, I believe, discovered and made available to readers a way of re-experiencing their and our worlds as multiple, serial phenomena of a richness and intensity so strong that one's response would perforce be an erotic one.

Whitman's Democratic Legacy Is Uneven

Michael Frank

Michael Frank is a literary critic and short story writer who has published in the New York Times, *the* Los Angeles Times Book Review, *and the* Yale Review, *among other publications.*

In the following selection, Frank reviews an exhibit celebrating the 150th anniversary of the first edition of Leaves of Grass *(1855) that focuses on the work's "spiritual message," "homosexual aspects," and "its author's racial views." He considers Walt Whitman's contradictory positions in each of these areas in order to reevaluate his legacy as a democratic poet. Most notably, Frank underscores Whitman's "undeniable racism" and hesitancy to support the abolitionist movement as an indication that his appreciation of the common person was not as all-encompassing as many have assumed. The image of Whitman as a carefree and spontaneous poet is also called into question by several examples of his careful formatting and extensive revisions of his own work.*

Anniversary exhibitions built around the publication of an author's Major Work often have a dutiful air. Books in first and subsequent editions are prettily arranged in glass cases, along with relevant manuscripts, photographs and ephemera. And don't forget the lock of hair, neatly braided or twirled just so, supplying the illusion that the great man (or woman) is somehow just out of sight.

You blink and imagine the hair on the head, the head on the body, the writer sprung to life, asking, as we do, why this, why now, what other than a dot on a calendar has brought us all, squinting and reverent, into this dim, sober, marbled room?

To the credit of Isaac Gewirtz, curator of the Henry W. and Albert A. Berg Collection of English and American Literature at the New York Public Library, the exhibition he has mounted on the 150th anniversary of the first edition of Walt Whitman's "Leaves of Grass" is commemoration with a point of view. That is a good thing, because Whitman's poem is one of those literary mazes, with passages brilliant and tedious, through which it is possible to follow dozens if not hundreds of ideas. Even when the book is regarded merely as an object, with its nine (or more) separate editions and countless other issues in Whitman's lifetime alone, the story is a dense one.

So what is driving the show "I Am With You" other than the nice round number of years that have elapsed since July 4, 1855, when Whitman, a former schoolteacher, printer, journalist and editor, first published his bold, unruly and groundbreaking poem? Drawing on the library's extensive holdings, Mr. Gewirtz has put on display at least one copy of every authorized American edition of "Leaves," along with the separate collections of poetry that Whitman later incorporated into his work, which he expanded, rearranged and revised nearly until the day he died.

Three Neglected Aspects

He has opened these books to specific pages, written extensive labels and published an accompanying pamphlet, with the goal, he said in an interview, of bringing attention to three aspects of "Leaves" that he believes have gotten short shrift: the poem's spiritual message, its homosexual aspects and its author's racial views.

Through these themes, Mr. Gewirtz said, "I Am With You" endeavors to "modulate the image of Whitman as the 'good gray poet' and champion of democracy." Perhaps it doesn't matter so much that this cozy, fossilized view of Whitman is, by now, a bit of a straw man. Mr. Gewirtz brushes aside the straw and, to take the knottiest theme first, explains that salvation, in Whitman's spiritual journey, "inheres in the journeying itself" and "is a process of moment-to-moment awakening."

As ever with Whitman, the goal is an open, perceiving, feeling self; he was less interested in talking about God than "about his own Oneness experience."

Examples of Whitman's spirituality, thus defined, abound in the first edition of "Leaves" (in later editions he began to formulate different ideas about a personal deity):

> I have said that the soul is not more than
> the body,
>
> And I have said that the body is not more
> than the soul,
>
> And nothing, not God, is greater to one
> than one's-self is.

Or:

> I hear and behold God in every object, yet I
> understand God not in the least,
>
> Nor do I understand who there can be more
> wonderful than myself.
>
> (The spiritual invariably seems to bring out
> the most epigrammatic in the poet.)

Mr. Gewirtz interprets Whitman's abounding selffulness as being more Eastern than Western in sensibility. "The 'myself' of which Whitman speaks in such contexts," he writes, "is not the ego, but what the Hindu Vedas, Upanishads and other Eastern spiritual traditions call 'the higher self.'" Since Whitman "sees no distinction between inner and outer, all that exists is God, which makes 'God' an unnecessary concept."

The Homosexual Aspects

A summary of a summary hardly does anyone's thinking justice—but there is a compression to this reading that feels a bit hasty; perhaps ideas given by slant and snippet can feel no other way. The exhibition seems on much steadier ground when it seeks to convey Whitman's homosexuality, even if it has to look outside of "Leaves" (to diary entries and the first draft of a poem in which the object of Whitman's love, in later drafts changed to a woman, is expressly a man) for corroboration.

It is important to remember that Whitman on heterosexual sex was strikingly explicit for serious literary writing in his or anyone's time, most famously in "A Woman Waits for Me" ("I pour the stuff to start sons and daughters fit for These States—I press with slow rude muscle"), which belongs to "Enfans d'Adam," one of the titled sequences of poems clustered together in "Leaves."

Whitman was unprecedented, too, in the way he portrayed women as erotic beings (think of the woman in "Song of Myself" spying on naked male swimmers, a subject Whitman's friend Thomas Eakins later took for his painting "The Swimming Hole"), but he did not politicize heterosexuality the way he did homosexual "adhesiveness," and it is in this that Whitman is arguably at his most daring.

While the actual sexual language of the Calamus cluster of poems is less explicit than its heterosexual counterpart—"He ahold of my hand has completely satisfied me" is about as racy as it gets—and was written in an era when expressions of physical affection between men were not automatically categorized as homosexual, Whitman believed that the "manly love of comrades" was fundamental to a truly democratic America. Men loving men would promote equality, respect and mutual admiration and thereby do away with destructive exploitation and violence.

Men thus connected would cease exploiting one another and would "make the continent indissoluble." Interestingly—or is it naïvely?—he held to this belief even during the high carnage of the Civil War:

Affection shall solve the problems of Freedom yet;

Those who love each other shall become
invincible.

"I Am With You" takes its name from a line in the poem that came to be called "Crossing Brooklyn Ferry": "I am with you, you men and women of a generation, or ever so many generations hence." In titling his pamphlet essay, Mr. Gewirtz amends the line to "I Am With [Some of] You" and in this way underlines one of the more problematic aspects of Whitman's thinking and writing, his undeniable racism. Like [modernist poet] T.S. Eliot's anti-Semitism, Whitman's ideas about blacks present a granite-hard stumbling block, one to reckon with or (if you can) step around.

Paradoxical Racial Views

Here, as in many places, Whitman was a paradox, and held ideas that changed over the years. He wrote a poem in the voice of an angry slave ("The Sleepers") and another compassionately portraying an older female slave ("Ethiopia Saluting the Colors"), yet he also expressed sympathy for the plight of the slave owner. Because he believed that abolition would lead to an insuperable division and war in his beloved union, he was at the same time anti-abolition and antislavery.

But his racial views were not merely political. While in "Leaves" he cushioned his sentiments, as though intuiting their unpalatable nature, he was probably never more offputting and narrow-sighted than when it came to his conviction, expressed in writings published and unpublished, of the inferiority of blacks, whose "intellect and caliber" he most egregiously likened to those of "so many baboons."

Mr. Gewirtz's selection of books, manuscripts and photographs makes several ancillary, more contained points about Whitman and his poem. You can feel Whitman's experience as a printer and compositor, for example, in his cover design for the first edition of "Leaves," with its gilt-stamped tendriled letters and leaf, fern and flower motifs. You can see Whitman the endless reviser at work in many places, but most notably in "The Blue Book," a copy of the 1860–61 edition, thus named because it was bound in blue paper wrappers; this is the actual copy that Whitman marked up to prepare the 1867 edition.

Whitman the sly promoter of his own work and life surfaces in a manuscript titled "Analysis of Leaves of Grass"; supposedly by Richard Maurice Bucke, who published a biography of Whitman, the page on display, describing how British critics and readers appreciate Whitman's work better than their American counterparts, is actually in Whitman's hand.

The exhibition's photographs tell a poignant parallel story: Whitman young (or youngish) shimmers out of a daguerreotype made at the beginning of his career, and we watch him age through successive images, with an ever more lined face and smoky, thickening swirl of beard. There is an 1864 picture of the Knickerbockers Nine, a nod to Whitman's love of baseball. (He trenchantly said that it embodied the "snap, go, fling, of the American atmosphere.") And there is "Wounded Soldiers in Hospital," a Civil War–era photograph that sets a visual cue for one of the more compelling interludes in Whitman's biography, the four years he spent in Washington, where by his own estimate he nursed 80,000 to 100,000 of the war's wounded, an experience he summed up as "the greatest privilege and satisfaction" and "the most profound lesson in my life."

And that lock of hair? It was most likely cut by Whitman himself; certainly he identified it on one side of its mounting, "Walt Whitman/America—Oct. 29 1891" and on the other, "A lock of hair/WW 73d year."

Bent into a tiny, tidy wreath, it has a surprising amount of gold in it for a fellow his age. But for Whitman, of all writers, this corporeal token seems hugely beside the point. As he wrote in a late contribution to "Leaves":

This is no book;

Who touches this, touches a man.

Whitman Took a Proslavery Position in His First Novel

Martin Klammer

Martin Klammer is professor of English and Africana Studies at Luther College in Decorah, Iowa. His writings include Whitman, Slavery, and the Emergence of "Leaves of Grass."

Walt Whitman's racial attitudes are a point of strong contention among scholars and critics. In the following excerpt, Klammer surveys the debate between African American critics in the 1950s before performing a reading of Whitman's first novel—the temperance tale Franklin Evans, or The Inebriate *(1842)—that highlights the author's racist, proslavery sentiments. Klammer places these attitudes in the context of Whitman's social and intellectual circle and suggests that Whitman constructed his stereotypical image of blacks from the popular literature of his day. Klammer concludes that, while Whitman would later revise his views, especially in* Leaves of Grass 1855, Franklin Evans *provides a valuable and somewhat startling insight into Whitman's early support of slavery in America.*

On July 4, 1953, Langston Hughes published a column on Walt Whitman in the popular African American newspaper, the *Chicago Defender*. In the column, subtitled "Calls Whitman Negroes' First Great Poetic Friend, Lincoln of Letters," Hughes praised Whitman as the "greatest of American poets," one whom "Negroes should read and remember." *Leaves of Grass*, Hughes wrote, "contains the greatest poetic statements of the real meaning of democracy ever made on our shores." Hughes cited passages from Whitman's poetry that

Martin Klammer, "Introduction and Chapter 1, 'The Construction of a Pro-Slavery Apology,'" in *Whitman, Slavery, and the Emergence of "Leaves of Grass."* University Park: Pennsylvania State University Press, 1995, pp. 1–26. All rights reserved. Reproduced by permission.

denounce slavery and proclaim the equality of all people; he asserted of a passage from the poem "Says" that "certainly there has been no clearer statement made on equality or civil or political rights than this statement"; and he noted the numerous references in Whitman's poetry "to Negroes, to Africa, to Asiatics and to darker peoples in general," all of whom Whitman includes within "the amplitude of his democracy and his humility."

Two weeks later Hughes printed in its entirety a letter from Lorenzo D. Turner, a professor of English at Roosevelt College in Chicago, who disagreed with Hughes's praise of Whitman's racial attitudes. Turner wrote: "From a careful study of all Whitman's published works I am convinced that he was not a friend of the Negro, and had very few contacts with Negroes, and thought that they were inferior to other human beings." Turner quoted a number of passages, mostly drawn from Whitman's journalism, in which Whitman attacked abolitionists, proposed a colonization scheme for blacks, admired the South and proslavery Senator John C. Calhoun, and expressed his reluctance to endorse Northern interference with the institution of slavery. Turner concluded: "*Leaves of Grass* was Whitman's show-piece, and, unfortunately, is the only one of his works that the average readers see. But to get a true picture of Whitman one has to read his writings that are not included in *Leaves of Grass*."

In another two weeks, Hughes responded with a column entitled "Like Whitman, Great Artists Are Not Always Good People." Turner's "provocative letter," Hughes wrote, "still does not deter me from maintaining that *Leaves of Grass* is a very great book, and one which Negroes or anyone else, for that matter, should read and remember." It is by Whitman's poems that "the whole world knows him," and his poems "came out of the greatest of the man himself." If Whitman in his "workaday editorials" contradicted "his own highest ideals"—as did [Thomas] Jefferson, the owner of slaves—then it is "the best of him that we choose to keep and cherish, not his worst," Hughes said. Many great artists and leaders "have not always been great men and women in their every day thoughts, speech or ways of living." Great people, Hughes said, are not gods: "They are mortal human beings, subjected to all the currents and evils, sins and stupidities of their times."

Whitman's Attitudes Toward Blacks

This simple exchange of letters in 1953 effectively captures the variety of Whitman's statements and the critical debate that has ensued as scholars and biographers seek to understand Whitman's baffling and seemingly contradictory attitudes toward African Americans. Commentators have repeatedly noted what Newton Arvin once called Whitman's "vacillations and inconsistencies on the slavery question." On one hand Whitman *is* as Hughes said, the great champion of democracy and equality, one who in *Leaves of Grass* consistently includes blacks and other people of color in his vision of an ideal republic and one who has had an enormous influence on African American poets. According to George Hutchinson, "Probably no white American poet has had a greater impact upon black American literature than Walt Whitman." But on the other hand, a number of Whitman texts show that he thought blacks inferior to whites and that his opposition to the extension of slavery had little, if anything, to do with sympathy for slaves.

Over the years critics have described and tried to account for Whitman's contradictions between his conservative, prejudiced views as a journalist, rooted in the mainstream Northern attitudes of his day, and his visionary, egalitarian ideas as a poet, inspired by the hope of a multiracial and inclusive America. Yet none has understood this polarity as a *historical* phenomenon—something that evolves in response both to historical events and to other contemporary discourses on sla-

Langston Hughes photographed in Harlem, New York, in 1958. Hughes exalted Walt Whitman for evoking the highest of democratic ideals in his poetry, despite acknowledging that Whitman, being human, did not always live up to those ideals. © Robert W. Kelley/Time & Life Pictures/Getty Images.

very—nor have critics described the convergence of these forces in Whitman's initial and revolutionary work, the 1855 *Leaves of Grass*. . . .

Race in Whitman's First Novel

Most discussions of Whitman's attitudes toward African Americans begin with his journalism of the late 1840s in which he opposed the extension of slavery into the new western territories. But such approaches overlook a much earlier text and what is by far Whitman's longest writing involving an African American: the eight curious chapters of the 1842 temperance novel *Franklin Evans, or The Inebriate* (hereafter *Franklin Evans*), written when Whitman was twenty-three. Briefly summarized, in this part of the novel the narrator, Franklin Evans, a young, alcoholic Northerner, travels south from New York to a Virginia plantation. Almost immediately upon arrival he is sexually attracted to a female Creole slave. Franklin lets his desire be known to the slave owner, and, in a fit of drunkenness (and with the slave owner's help), he marries the woman and simultaneously has her manumitted [freed from slavery]. Upon sobering up he discovers to his disgust what has happened, but he is "saved" from his own actions by the sudden appearance of a sexually aggressive Northern white woman who, after arriving on the plantation, targets him as her next romantic conquest. The Creole wife then becomes violently jealous and in a mad frenzy murders the woman and commits suicide, leaving young Franklin to ponder—and reject—any sense of responsibility.

Whitman was not especially proud of *Franklin Evans*, telling [American journalist] Horace Traubel that it was "damned rot—rot of the worst sort" and claiming that he wrote it in three days with "the help of a bottle of port or what not." Yet it was by far Whitman's most popular work, selling in his estimation around twenty thousand copies. Most critics agree with Whitman that the novel is a hackneyed piece of tractarian temperance fiction, and yet the absence of critical commentary about the unusual "Creole episode" is surprising. What critical discussions there are of *Franklin Evans* often ignore, or at the very least minimize, the issues of race in the novel. The few commentators who speak at all about the mulatto narrative in *Franklin Evans* treat it as a sexual rites-of-passage for young Franklin (and, by association, for Whitman) apart from any considerations of race. What is missing from all of these discussions are essential issues: why, for example, one-fourth of Whitman's temperance novel is devoted to a biracial relationship, or how that portion of the narrative allows the speaker—and perhaps Whitman, too, through the writing of fiction—to pursue sexual fantasies about a slave woman within the bounds of conventional Victorian morality, using bouts of alcoholism as a psychic and moral "cover" for his desire, manipulation, and domination of the woman. Moreover, *Franklin Evans* is singularly revealing not only in what it indicates about a young Walt Whitman's racial attitudes, but especially about how these attitudes are constructed from an eclectic gathering of various "texts" and ideologies then prevalent in both Northern *and* Southern antebellum culture. Most revealing is the way in which Whitman replicates the conventions of pro-slavery fiction and subverts those of abolitionist literature to create a thoroughgoing apology for slavery, all within a temperance tract. On one hand, Whitman's essentially pro-slavery posture is not entirely surprising, given the predominant racial attitudes of the nineteenth century when most white Americans viewed persons of African descent as inferior beings and, in the words of historian George Fredrickson, as a "permanently alien and unassimilable element of the population." Yet the very presence of the Creole episode in *Franklin Evans* is striking when one considers both the expectations or Whitman's reform-minded audience—sympathizers of abolition as well as temperance—and the absence of any need for such an episode.

Conventional Discourse on Race

Moreover, *Franklin Evans* was published during a period of relative calm in the history of the volatile slavery question in antebellum America. For many Americans, slavery had simply not yet become an issue. The constitutional compromises and the 1820 Missouri Compromise appeared to have settled the disputes between North and South for the time being. *Franklin Evans* suggests not only Whitman's heightened interest in race relations but also a direct relationship between Whitman's racial attitudes and his reliance on conventional discursive strategies, a relationship that remains constant from early in his career through the publication of the 1855 *Leaves of Grass*. The conventionality of Whitman's racial prejudices is reflected in the degree to which Whitman borrows from other discourses to create his own discourse—that is, the degree to which his text is constructed of other texts. So long as his own racial attitudes reflect the racial prejudices of a mainstream segment of American culture, his discursive strategies will largely be the imitation of what he has seen and read. In other words, his discursive strategies will always be as orthodox as his racial assumptions. When Whitman begins to liberate himself, he does so simultaneously with respect to both race and rhetoric: his radical new thinking about blacks demands radical new discursive strategies, and vice versa. . . . A close and contextualized reading of his most popular work suggests that nowhere is Whitman more conventional or more racist, even by nineteenth-century standards, than in *Franklin Evans*. . . .

One should not altogether be surprised by the text's proslavery stance and formulaic approaches to race, however, especially considering the types of racial thinking within Whitman's political circles, his personal experience with blacks, and his history as a writer up until this time. Although the Democratic response to slavery was by no means monolithic, most Jacksonian Democrats enthusiastically asserted white superiority and argued for black exclusion from political life. Sociologist Pierre van den Berghe has termed this ideology as "Herrenvolk democracy"—that is, the equal superiority of all who belong to the Herrenvolk (master race) over all who do not. Thus, Jacksonian democratic ideology carried the rhetoric of popular democracy to an extreme "almost unparalleled in American political history," according to George Fredrickson, and at the same time condoned a form of "anti-Negro demagoguery that anticipated the Southern race baiters of a later era." This pattern was especially apparent in Whitman's home state of New York, where, Fredrickson says, "extreme disparagement of local blacks was often combined with fervent assertions of Jacksonian principle." Even the most radical spokespersons for the common laborer, including those associated with Workingmen's movements, emphasized that democracy was for whites only.

The combination of Northern white egalitarianism and black proscription was more than rhetoric. In 1821 the suffrage of blacks in New York was constitutionally restricted to those who owned at least $250 of property. The measure was initiated by the state's Democrats and chiefly supported by voters who feared black economic competition and wanted to make the state unattractive to African American immigration. Moreover, there is considerable evidence that during the rise of radical egalitarianism in New York in the 1830s Jacksonians used anti-black prejudice as a weapon against their Whig opponents. As John Ashworth has tersely put it: "The Democratic commitment to racism was almost as intense as the Democratic commitment to democracy." Not only Democrats held such views. George Fredrickson asserts that after the 1830s "widespread, almost universal agreement" existed on the beliefs that blacks were intellectually and temperamentally inferior to whites and that full equality for blacks in the foreseeable future was virtually unthinkable. In this context, Whitman's portrayal of [Creole slave] Margaret in *Franklin Evans* is hardly surprising.

Little Actual Contact with Blacks

Whitman's own lack of actual experience with blacks surely contributed to his naive and stereotypical views. Whitman's contact with African Americans, like that of most white Northerners at the time, was extremely limited. . . .

Without any firsthand knowledge of blacks, then, Whitman constructed images and stories of them culled from popular literature, a source he had turned to frequently in his early career as a writer. . . .

Without belaboring the obvious, he was an immature writer. And yet the particular choices he makes in his first foray into writing about race suggest both a heightened awareness or interest in issues of race and a pro-slavery position whose themes and strategies were largely taken from Southern literature.

Franklin Evans locates young Walt Whitman as deeply embedded in popular conventions of writing and racial thinking. How Whitman would become an original writer, how he would develop the startling voice of the 1855 *Leaves of Grass*, has much to do with the liberation of his vision and writing about blacks and slavery. In the next four years (1842–46) Whitman worked for several New York-area newspapers but had little to say about blacks or slavery as compromise agreements between North and South were not contested. With American victory in the war with Mexico in 1846, however, questions about the extension of slavery into the new territories once again thrust the issue onto the nation's center stage. Whitman's passionate involvement in these questions began in response to heated debates in Congress that would not be resolved until 1850, and then only tentatively.

The Nazis Reshaped Whitman's Democratic Themes with Their Own Message

Walter Grünzweig

Walter Grünzweig, author of Constructing the German Whitman, *is a professor of American studies at the Dortmund University of Technology (Technische Universität Dortmund) in Germany.*

In the following viewpoint, Grünzweig investigates the Nazi appropriation of Walt Whitman's life and works. Grünzweig notes that Nazi critics reshaped Whitman's use of terms such as people, race, *and* blood *and misread his Civil War poetry as a celebration of warfare to fit their own genocidal purposes. These practices led to the emergence in the 1930s of a group of German "worker poets" who modeled their poems on Whitman's plain style and sympathies for the working class but lacked Whitman's disdain for social elites. Grünzweig is careful to point out, however, that such use of Whitman's themes and techniques by the Third Reich should not lead people to believe that he would have supported their aims in any way.*

There were attempts by critics operating during the Nazi period to make use of Whitman. After the Nazi takeover, the right-wing Whitmanite Heinrich Lersch (see below) was once asked whether he thought Whitman could be of use for National Socialist ideology. He shrewdly replied that he thought Whitman would have a lot to say to the Nazi period if the word "democracy" were replaced by "Volk" ([the German word for the] people) wherever it appeared, implying that there were dimensions to Whitman's poetry that could indeed appeal to Nazi ears, a statement that would be shocking to most Whitmanites, both inside Germany and outside.

In the *Volkserzisher* (Educator of the People), a radical anti-Semitic journal which was in its thirty-seventh year in the year the Nazis took power, one Heinrich Kästner wrote an article entitled "Walt Whitman, the Prophet of a New Humanity," shortly after Hitler had come to power: "Already in the last century, a man of rare greatness departed from the course determined by machines, technology, and capitalism, which humanity still follows today. It was a man who anticipated centuries of human development and became a prophet of a future race." The antimodernist impulse characteristic of National Socialist ideology and strategy is the driving force of Kästner's article. Even the typical pseudorevolutionary anticapitalist rhetoric appears prominently. Dissatisfied with "machines, technology, and capitalism," but not really interested in revolution, Nazi ideologues searched for "solutions" to the general human dissatisfaction with modern life. Such solutions always pointed to the past, even if they were said to anticipate future centuries. "Whitman restores to humans an open mind for everything that is alive and gives them the energy and strength to manage their life and their death. This unique person [Whitman] has deeply felt the divine character of a fully lived life which man has abandoned and turned into a servant of his daily needs." Through the replacement of this divine feeling of life (referring to the individual's mystical relationship to the *Volk* and to the environment) by the intellect and through its functionalization in a technological environment, humans have destroyed their "pure relationships of their lives to the world and to things." Through the demystifying methods of science, "man" has embarked in a wrong direction.

The mystical-irrational dimension Nazis took over from Christian religion was used in very rational and calculating ways, as is obvious in such quotations. To complete this microcosm of National Socialist ideology, Kästner ends his Whitman essay (in which the term "democracy" does not appear) with a sentence that could hardly have been misunderstood in May 1933: "We do believe in a perfect human race exemplified by one man." Whitman as Führer?

Intentionally Misrepresented

Some six years later, Hans Flasche undertook an investigation of the "German spirit in the Anglo-Saxon philosophy of history." Although he pretended to retain academic objectivity when analyzing the foundations of Whitman's philosophy, passages like the following are all too close to official Nazi diction: "[Whitman's] immediate intuition of vital values strongly emphasizes nature, *Volk*, race, blood, soil as important forces. Whitman has a high estimation of the individualism of a person, but he always places the individual in the community of the *Volk*." This passage contains key terms of the National Socialist ideological rhetoric that had become fully integrated into public German discourse by 1939. For the misinterpretation of Whitman along Nazi lines, the perverted use of such terms as "people," "race," or "blood" was a prerequisite. There is nothing wrong with such terms unless they signal intolerance, repression, and inhumanity. Integrated in the biologistic universe of Nazi ideology, even a poet like Whitman could become the victim of a perverted reading and turn into an unwitting accomplice of Nazi aims.

Another interesting misrepresentation concerns Whitman's stand on war. Whitman's war poetry was so remarkable because it was in essence pacifist war poetry (supported biographically through his work as a nurse). Flasche puts it in different terms:

Man and woman should not remain confined in their limited individuality. They must always be conscious that they are descendants, links in a long chain, that they beget and bear children and thereby maintain the racial and folkish values. The highest racial values that are passed on include bravery, valor, heroism. Those who gave their lives for the Fatherland must be accorded unanimous gratitude. From their graves, energy rises for new deeds. The memory of the sons who shed their blood for the fatherland is the holiest legacy of a people, even holier, in some ways, than national literature and art.

The way in which the scholar of literature belittles the value of his craft in comparison with the warring caste is touching—and entirely appropriate to the time the essay was published, at the beginning of World War II. But the quotation also shows why such a perverted reading of Whitman remained an exception: while the terms and some of the concepts used here *can* be found in his poetry, they go against the tenor of the *oeuvre* [work] as a whole. As Whitman states in "As I Ponder'd in Silence," *Leaves* is concerned mostly with war *"for the Body and for the eternal Soul"*. The direct National Socialist claim upon Whitman was doomed because it reflected neither the spirit nor the text of the American.

The German Worker Poets

The various attempts to recruit Whitman for German nationalism and Nazism could be overlooked as mere aberrations were it not for an indirect impact Whitman had on Nazi culture which is much more significant: the Whitmanesque poetry of some of the so-called *Arbeiterdichter* (worker poets). Although this is arguably a case of creative reception involving Whitman's adaptation in German literature, its function is so blatantly ideological that it needs to be discussed [here].

The ongoing discussion among German critics and literary historians about whether there is a literature specifically relating to the working class, a proletarian literature, has also dealt with the question of whether this literature is by, for, or about workers. The group of writers we are concerned with here were, technically speaking, workers, at least for a time. Their thinking and identity, however, betray a lower-middle-class background—their "fall" into the working class was the result of impoverishment. Their intended audience was not primarily workers but the middle class; the theme of their writing was usually related to work, to the living conditions and environment of workers—but with a special twist.

The political background of these poets is diverse: some were anti-Marxist from the very start, others came from the Social Democratic Party, but none of them were leftists in a strict sense. They abhorred naturalist writing of the kind produced by [Émile] Zola, [Gerhart] Hauptmann, [Arno] Holz, or [Johannes] Schalf as "poetry for paupers." They especially rejected the concept of class struggle, which to them was defensive and apologetic. Rather than fighting for a classless society, they demanded social recognition of workers and their acceptance into (bourgeois) society.

A New/Old Worker Identity

It should be remembered that the official name of the Nazi Party was Nationalsozialistische Deutsche Arbeiter Partei (National Socialist German Workers' Party). The Nazis, although extreme anti-Marxists, did call themselves socialist and did define their roots as working class. In their rhetoric, they were also "anticapitalist," although not in the Marxist sense, but in the context of their anti-"plutocratic" and anti-Semitic world view.

According to Nazi ideology, it was Marxists together with "capitalists" who had degraded the proud German worker to the status of a "proletarian" without any feeling of self-esteem. The solution to the "question" of the worker offered by the Nazis was mainly psychological: workers had to adopt a new identity; society, rather than looking down on workers as members of a lower class, had to accept them as important and equal members of the community. In this way, the actual reasons for social degradation, human alienation, and economic impoverishment of the working class, which derived from the industrialized and technologized society, were obscured. Nazi ideology carefully and skillfully appealed to the psychological dissatisfaction of an impoverished class, suggesting that the solution to their problems lay in a return to old values. Essentially, they promised workers a return to their former preindustrial status as artisans.

Capitalism, therefore, was not to be overthrown, but educated. The representatives of "international high finance" such as Jews or Freemasons needed to be "weeded out" and replaced by a class of truly German "employers" who would accord due recognition to workers, treat them "fairly," and pay them "honest" wages. This solidarity was to emerge from a shared feeling of nationhood; the fact that all members of the society were Germans was to ensure mutual benevolence.

A "National Community"

The *Arbeiterdichter* had independently arrived at these very same conclusions. Most of them, including the two figures discussed in greater detail here—Heinrich Lersch and Karl Bröger—reacted enthusiastically to World War I. They welcomed the general national fraternization expressed in the emperor's announcement that he knew no more parties (and classes), but only Germans. At the beginning of the war, Bröger wrote a poem whose final five lines became famous throughout Germany:

We always have loved you

but never called it love.

But your greatest peril revealed in a splendid
way

that your poorest son was also your most
faithful one

Be aware of this, o Germany.

Pathos-laden, this poem imploringly demands that German
society, which in the face of the war crisis had been saved by
the German worker, by "the poorest" but "most faithful son"
of the nation, reaccept workers into the national community
(*Volksgemeinschaft*).

For the *Arbeiterdichter*, the idea of a national community
and simultaneous abolition of class barriers (as naive as this
may sound) was not just a wartime necessity but also a peace-
time ideal. "Denk es, O Deutschland" not only means "Be
aware of it" but also "Do not forget." After the war, these poets believed, the country should be restructured using the
model of the army. The ideal of a pseudo-classless national
community should be extended to the work place. They demanded a "work community" (*Werkgemeinschaft*) which would
ensure social *inclusion*, rather than *exclusion* of workers. To
National Socialist critics, this was welcomed as the "break-
through of the [German] worker to his people." Workers
would again be able to "experience" what it means to be a
part of their nation; the work they render for their nation
would thereby acquire new meaning.

Using Whitman to Mythicize Work

In reality, of course, this did not remove the alienating and
frustrating work conditions that laborers were subjected to.
No factory in Nazi Germany was closed down and converted
into a craftshop. Quite to the contrary, the Nazi takeover, due
to the increase in military production, sped up technological
progress. Therefore, in addition to creating a fictitious harmony between the classes, it was also necessary to instill in
workers' minds the belief that their work was not alienating
and degrading, even if in effect it was. This required a mythi-

cization of work—turning the steel worker into a blacksmith, the textile worker into a tailor, and so forth—that is, recreating the earlier guild spirit by using its diction, although its basis had long disappeared in the course of industrialization. A poetry that performed all of these ideological tasks would seem to be hopelessly overtaxed. Unless, of course, one had Walt Whitman as a model. . . .

The line leading from Whitman to the *Arbeiterdichter* and, finally, to the Third Reich should not be exaggerated. Whitman, certainly, cannot be held responsible for being used by poets like Lersch and Bröger whose poems ended up in the songbooks of the Hitler youth. Parallels exist predominantly in the rhetoric (masses, collectivism, community). Whitman's mode of addressing individual professions was a significant lyrical parallel to the corporate ideal of the National Socialists, who preferred to divide their society horizontally into labor groups rather than admit to the reality of a vertical class division. The mythicization of labor and work place could not eliminate class antagonisms and alienation, but it could make them appear irrelevant for a time. Whitman's nature mysticism and his rejection of traditional religiosity fit Hitler's myth of *Vorsehung* (providence). Whitman's emphasis on the physical character of humans and nature resonated with Nazi slogans of *Blut und Boden* (blood and soil). Whitman's idealistic *Pathos* and his praise of motherhood also were echoed by Nazis. Even in Bröger's cycle of poems entitled "Phallos," published in the "monthly for the future of German culture," *Die Tat* (The Deed), Diederichs, its German-nationalist conservative publisher, was able to see the signs of a new race, "as it will once be reborn in the Germanic spirit." The stagnation in German Whitman reception in the years since the end of World War II is a result not only of the general distrust of *Pathos* in literature and the other arts, but also of the uneasiness caused by the many specific parallels between Whitman's poetry and that of the National Socialist songbooks.

A Mistrust of Whitmanesque Poetry

Even the many German exiles who wanted to use Whitman as an ally in the antifascist struggle were confused by a *Pathos* which reminded them all too often of the propagandistic discourse of the system from which they had escaped. Klaus Mann, Thomas's son, idolized Whitman, and, in 1941, authored a long article on "The Present Greatness of Walt Whitman," attempting to prove that Whitman would have taken an antiisolationist anti-Nazi stand and would have wanted the United States to join the allied powers. Yet even he, one of the most enthusiastic German Whitman admirers, had to admit to himself:

> We have learned to be more skeptical and restrained about the "splendid day-rise of science" and the magnificent modernism of our enlightened age. Nor do we share any more Whitman's exuberant admiration for everything colossal— masses of men, masses of land, masses of steel or water or words. The cruel experiences of our times are more likely to teach us that neither *quantity* nor technical *progress* as such have any moral value; that everything depends upon the spirit in which they are to be employed. They may be employed "for the sake of the Soul," or for the sake of evil and destruction.

> What seems to be the weakest spot in his philosophy is his way of simplifying the character of man and of ignoring the elements of madness and infamy so profoundly inherent in human nature.

The "cruel experiences of our times"—and the cruel sounds and rhetoric that time produced. German readers had become uncertain about Whitmanesque poetry in the course of the Third Reich and this has remained true until the present.

Whitman's Views Earned Him Scorn from the Proslavery Press

Eric Conrad

Eric Conrad is managing editor of the Walt Whitman Quarterly Review.

While several scholars have identified examples of Walt Whitman's racist attitudes in his works, especially those produced before Leaves of Grass *in 1855, it is also true that he was ridiculed for his perceived sympathy for slaves by proslavery publications in both the North and the South during the 1850s and 1860s. In the following viewpoint, Conrad provides examples of such attacks, citing passages from the northern publication* New York Day Book *and the southern* Daily Delta *that use racist and proslavery rhetoric to denounce* Leaves of Grass *as nonsense intended to elicit empathy for the "uncivilized" slave population. Such reviews, however, were deftly utilized by Whitman's abolitionist publishers to promote the work to readers who did not support slavery.*

A previously uncollected review of the 1860 *Leaves of Grass* appeared in the *New York Day Book* on June 9, 1860. Nathaniel R. Stimson founded the *Day Book* in 1848 to "promote the proslavery cause among New York City's commercial interests." The periodical billed itself as the "White Man's Paper" and even briefly changed its name to the *Caucasian* while under the control of John H. Van Evrie and Rushmore G. Horton. As [Whitman's publishers] Thayer & Eldridge were promoting the third edition of *Leaves of Grass*, Van Evrie was preparing and advertising his most notorious work, *Negroes and Negro Slavery: The First an Inferior Race: The Latter Its Normal Condition* (1861), which championed the notion of "subgenation," a term van Evrie coined for the "natural or normal relation of an inferior to a superior race." As Martin Klammer notes, Van Evrie's writings appealed "to part of the same audience that Whitman was always hoping to reach: socially insecure whites in search of a sense of identity that could help make the existing social and economic systems more tolerable." When Whitman's radical abolitionist publishers turned to Van Evrie's copperhead [antiwar northern Democrat] newspaper for a review of the 1860 *Leaves of Grass*, they knew a warm reception was unlikely, despite the fact that Whitman and the *Day Book* targeted some of the same readers.

An Unorthodox Promotional Strategy

In their May 24, 1860, letter to Whitman, Thayer & Eldridge notified the poet that they had distributed review copies of *Leaves of Grass* (via Henry Clapp Jr.) to New York's "Editorial Fraternity," a politically diverse group of periodicals which included Clapp's *Saturday Press*, Van Evrie's *Day Book*, James Gordon Bennett's *New York Herald*, Horace Greeley's *New York Tribune*, and J. Warner Campbell's *New York Illustrated News*. Earlier in March, Clapp had suggested exactly this plan: distribute *Leaves of Grass* to New York's most popular newspapers regardless of their likely responses. Thayer & Eldridge eventually took Clapp's advice, expressing their hopes to Whitman that *Leaves of Grass* would have a "strong effect" upon the editors of these periodicals, "readers who command the Press." The "effect" on the *Day Book* was indeed "strong": *Leaves of Grass* was denounced as the "maddest folly and the merest balderdash that ever was written." Van Evrie's disgust in the *Day Book* over Thayer & Eldridge's new volume would have been fairly predictable considering both parties' respective political allegiances. The *Day Book*'s attack on Whitman channels these acute political differences, incorporating pro-slavery rhetoric aimed at abolitionists like Thayer & Eldridge who defended what Van Evrie argued was a degraded and ani-malistic negro population. Thus, Van Evrie's Whitman is a poet "disfigured by the most disgusting beastiality [sic]," a "great strong, filthy bull, delighting alike in his size and his strength, and his filth." If Van Evrie's appraisal of *Leaves of Grass* fails to astonish, Thayer & Eldridge's attempt to drum up publicity for Whitman by soliciting hostile critics like the *Day Book* should likewise come as no surprise given the publishers' unorthodox promotional strategies. For example, *Leaves of Grass Imprints*, Thayer & Eldridge's ambitious, 64-page pamphlet advertising the 1860 edition, reprints several vitriolic reviews of Whitman and his poetry, the same kind of material an appeal to the *Day Book* was apt to produce. Here is the review as it appeared in the *New York Day Book*:

LEAVES OF GRASS. Boston: Thayer & Eldridge. Year 85 of the States—(1860–61)

This is a new edition of the work of Walt Whitman, which some years ago created so great a sensation both in this country and abroad, and it seems now destined to renew the former effect. It is very much discussed and criticized, and is indeed a singular production. Distinguished by power of a certain sort, by bursts of originality, by occasional undoubted cleverness, it is also disfigured by the most disgusting beasti-ality we remember ever to have seen in print; a beastiality which is the most prominent feature of the book, which is utterly animal, and so marked that it not only gives tone to the work, but indicates the character of the writer. Vigorous, coarse, vulgar, indecent, powerful, like a great strong, filthy bull, delighting alike in his size and his strength, and his filth; full of egotism, rampant, but not insufferable, fully be-lieving himself to be a representative man and poet of the American people; persuaded that he is the great poet whose advent the world is waiting for, and that his errand is to sing his own individuality, his own peculiarities, whether physical or spiritual, but particularly physical; his own idiosyncracies, whether little or great; his own characteristics, whether noble or mean; and all these not so much because they are his individualities and characteristics and idiosyncracries, as because he thinks they typify those of other Americans—this is Walt Whitman's character and notions, as they seem to be developed in his Leaves of Grass. The measure in which he writes is his own, and is often no measure at all, but a sort of alliteratives [sic] style, with a certain rough music in it; his style is outside of all rules, transgresses, grammar and rhetoric, it jumbles up slang and vulgarity with choice language, huddles together English and scraps of French and Latin and Spanish in the absurdest fashion, and yet at times has a certain terseness that is telling. The book is, in many respects abominable; in many respects the maddest folly and the merest balderdash that ever was written; but it unfortunately possesses these streaks of talent, these grains of originality, which will probably preserve the author from oblivion. We should advise nobody to read it unless he were curious in literary monstrosities, and had a stomach capable of digesting the coarsest stuff ever offered by caterers for the reading public, and yet those who are catholic [i.e., having a universal outlook] enough to appreciate two grains of wheat hid in two bushels of chaff, will not be uninterested in the volume.

Southern Critics Attack

On June 25, 1860, Whitman's name reappears in the *Day Book* in an excerpt from the New Orleans *Daily Delta* (1845–1863), a newspaper that paid considerable attention to Whitman in the summer of 1860. Following Clapp's insistence, Thayer & Eldridge made sure copies of *Leaves of Grass* penetrated the offices of New York's most prominent papers—even Van Evrie's *Day Book*—but Whitman's publishers were reluctant (perhaps even unable) to engage a Southern readership in the same way. As [editor of the *Virginia Quarterly Review*] Ted

Genoways has shown, Thayer & Eldridge—constricted by laws banning anti-slavery literature and suspected in Alabama of disseminating abolitionist propaganda through their book agents—were plagued by a "near-total inability to sell books in the South." The following previously undocumented review from the *Daily Delta* criticizes Thayer & Eldridge for refusing to introduce *Leaves of Grass* to the South and assaults Whitman with thinly veiled racist invective. Here is the article as it first appeared in the *Daily Delta* on June 17, 1860:

WALT WHITMAN

There is an unkempt, uncouth poet of New York, or rather of Brooklyn, whose name on earth, in secular parlance, is Walt Whitman. The Cincinnati Commercial calls him the "Yahoo of American literature." Judging from specimens of his jargonic poetry, which we have seen, (his publishers have not sent the lately published volume of his "Leaves of Grass" to the South;) we think the Commercial scarcely does justice to his peculiar merits in calling him a Yahoo. We think rather that he can claim a comparison with the gorilla, one of the peculiarities of which is to pile up chunks of wood, in rude imitation of the house-building of his Ethiopian neighbors, but without having the slightest idea of making a house or any other rational object in view. Just so does Walt Whitman seem to pile up words. If they mean nothing, it is all the same. Something and nothing are one, according to the Brahmic [Hindu] theory which this nondescript poet appears to have borrowed from the mystic sage of Concord, Ralph Waldo Emerson. Emerson says that Leaves of Grass gave him "great and unspeakable inward joy." We can almost envy the sage's vegetarian appetite, and can find no limit to our admiration for his powers of digestion. We don't object to salad, indeed, rather affect it, when served up according to true gastronomic art. But we confess that we can't readily take to grass, literal or metaphorical, when pulled up by the roots and tossed to us with a pitchfork as if we were a hungry herbivorous beast.

Walt Whitman has evidently fallen into the mistake of many strong-natured, egotistical and unbalanced men, of supposing that to despise the graces, amenities, and conventions of art is the more fully to place themselves in sympathy with nature. They forget that there is only a verbal, not an unverbal distinction between nature and art, and that the grandest and the most trivial things done by man in the way of art are as natural as falling dew or blooming flowers.

The connections the *Daily Delta* draws among the "Ethiopian," "the gorilla," and Whitman would have appealed to readers of the *Day Book*, especially those sympathetic with Van Evrie's pseudo-scientific theories of race. Though Van Evrie would insist that God created "the Negro" and "the Caucasian" separately, the *Delta*'s racist parody shares with the author of *Negroes and Negro Slavery* a discourse that placed the Ethiopian—what Van Evrie calls "the isolated negro of Africa"—at the base of humanity, the "last and least, the lowest in the scale but possibly the first in order of Creation." For crude comedic effect, the *Delta*'s lampoon of Whitman ostensibly allows Van Evrie's "lowest" to occupy the most sophisticated position in the brief prose sketch, though the African's proximity to the gorilla insures that readers will not confuse the Ethiopian for a more "civilized" species. Whereas the Ethiopian can build a house with a "rational object in view," the gorilla can only perform a "rude imitation" of his neighbor. Whitman and his "jargonic poetry," in imitating the gorilla (whose base instincts mimic the Ethiopian), rest at the bottom of the *Delta*'s evolutionary scale. The *Day Book* racializes Whitman through repeated references to his "beastiality," but the *Delta* makes literal Van Evrie's implication, subordinating Whitman to both the Ethiopian and the gorilla, coloring all three with a culturally legible black-face.

The *Delta*'s Parody of Whitman

As proof that they are not "exaggerating Walt Whitman's oddities as a poet," the *Daily Delta* then reprints "Poemet" from the *New York Saturday Press* as an example of "the least rhapsodic and ragged, and least unintelligible" of the poet's compositions. Following "Poemet" is the *Delta's* own parody of Whitman reprinted below:

> If Walt Whitman had occasion to put forth his notions of poetry and poets in dithyrambic form, we can well imagine the strain to run in this wise:
>
> If a great poet thinks he sings, and sings not,
>
> Very good!
>
> Or if a great poem thinks it's sung, and the great poet
>
> who sung it never lived nor loved, nor was married
>
> to immortal verse or to a human female, nor
>
> drank brandy, nor chewed tobacco, nor stimulated
>
> his brain with coffee,
>
> Very good also!
>
> Or if the great poem is sung, but thinks it's not sung,
>
> let it be content.
>
> Any way and every way, these are all dreams and all facts;
>
> These are all facts and all dreams;
>
> As dreamy and as factual as the mill between Heenan
>
> and Sayers, the Common Council, the Chicago

Convention, the Great Eastern, John Brown
and

the "irrepressible conflict."

All these things are equally something and
nothing,

Nothing and something.

Let them alone!

Come away!!

Pshaw!!!

But, to speak the truth that is in me, and in
you, too,

who are only a shadow of me, it is the sub-
lime

nihility of these things that inflates me with
poetic

emptiness—

Inflates me, myself, and not you, or Thomas,
Richard

or Henry—

Inflates me, I mean, and Emerson, who is
only another

mood of me—

Inflates us both, who are one, I say, and
causes us to

riot in a chaos of uninterpretable lingo, and
to shout

from empyrean height of unspeakable joy

Whoop-de dooden-doo!

The *Delta* concludes its critique of Whitman with excerpts from the *New York Albion* which again parody the poet and attack his work as "monstrous beyond belief." In the following weeks the *Delta* would return to Whitman again and again as a target of derision. On June 24, 1860, the *Delta* featured "A Specimen from Walt Whitman," which reprinted Whitman's "Manahatta," introduced by the following two paragraphs:

> Last Sunday we gave some inklings of Walt Whitman's style of poetry, the peculiar merit and charm of which, say the critics who have espoused his claims to unlimited Parnassian [Olympian] honors, consist in its lusty naturalness. There is a huge deal of cant and nonsense babbled about nature—some things being condemned summarily because unnatural, and other things approved unhesitatingly because natural. We would like to know, to begin with—and that involves the whole question—what is nature, or rather what, in the whole range of human thought and experience, is *not* nature. But we will not pause here to investigate the question.
>
> We will only say, for the benefit of those who are disposed to put inestimable store by Walt Whitman's lusty naturalness, that an alligator floundering in a slough, a hog wallowing in the mire, a buzzard plunging its beak into carrion, and many other objects of similar dignity, may all be lusty and natural, but not particularly sublime, beautiful, captivating, or even pleasant. We have no disposition to assert that Walt Whitman may not be lusty and natural. At least we are willing for his admirers to make the most of the proposition. It is not the thing itself—lusty naturalness—that is the subject of either esthetic or moral consideration, but the quality of the thing. And what is the quality of the thing, let the reader judge from one other specimen: ["Manahatta" is then reprinted followed by a missing passage.]

The *Delta*'s final appraisal of "Manahatta" remains a mystery—all available copies of the newspaper on microfilm are reproduced from an original which is missing the final paragraph.

Southern Critics Aid Whitman's Fame

Regardless of what that paragraph had to say about Whitman's work, the *Delta* did not dismiss the poet for long. The paper returned to Whitman again on July 15, 1860, in the appropriately titled "Walt Whitman Again." The bulk of the article consists of a lengthy *Vanity Fair* reprint, but the *Delta*'s short prose introduction to "The Torch-Bearer" is noteworthy as a record of Whitman's increasing public visibility in the heart of the South. The *Delta* writes:

> Whenever a promising vein of nonsense is opened, it is worked most industriously by the wags of literature. We all remember how, upon the appearance of [Henry Wadsworth] Longfellow's Hiawatha, the papers were filled with parodies of it; and how the intellectual ribs of the public were tickled with the innumerable burlesques that appeared.
>
> Walt Whitman is at present the rage. He is celebrated by many vagrant pens. Like [Shakespeare's] Falstaff, he is not only funny himself, but the cause of fun in others.
>
> The last effort to attain the height which this new author appears in the last number of Vanity Fair, and we reproduce it here in order that the lungs of our readers may be exercised by the moans of gentle and moderate cachination [sic]:

If Whitman was the laughing stock of the *Delta*, a source of "gentle and moderate cachination"—"not only funny himself, but the cause of fun in others"—he was so because his poetry was "the rage" in the summer of 1860. Thanks in part to Thayer & Eldridge's aggressive marketing strategy, which placed copies of *Leaves of Grass* in the hands of proslavery men like Van Evrie and comic journals like *Vanity Fair*, Whitman's notoriety was building in the South, an area his publishers were unable to access directly as the nation's "irrepressible conflict" became increasingly unavoidable.

Whitman's "Democratic Vistas" Is a Key to Understanding America

David Brooks

David Brooks is a New York Times *columnist and PBS News-Hour commentator. He has served in editorial roles at the* Wall Street Journal, *the* Atlantic Monthly, *and the* Weekly Standard.

Brooks argues in the following viewpoint that Walt Whitman's 1871 prose work "Democratic Vistas" is essential to understanding America in all its complexity. There may be inconsistencies in the essay and in Whitman's view of democracy, but the nation itself is founded on a paradox: it asserts the power of its government while also fostering individualism. Despite the bravado Whitman displays in "Democratic Vistas", he wrote it in the bleak aftermath of the Civil War, partly in response to attacks on the American system by the British historian Thomas Carlyle. Whitman maintained his optimism concerning America's future and its mission and continued to believe that the nation would bring forth many great poets and works long after he was gone.

Whenever I hear people say something stupid about America, which is often these days, I want to punch them in the nose and hand them Walt Whitman's 1871 essay "Democratic Vistas." The punch would temporarily stem the flow of idiocy, and the copy of "Democratic Vistas" would give them some accurate sense of what the United States is all about.

I should make it clear from the start that "Democratic Vistas" can be an infuriating piece of writing. Whitman could

David Brooks, "What Whitman Knew," *Atlantic Monthly*, May 2003, pp. 32–33. All rights reserved. Reproduced by permission.

not be bothered with mundane considerations like clarity, coherence and organizational logic. But it survives as our nation's most brilliant political sermon because it embodies the exuberant energy of American society—the energy that can make other peoples so nervous—and it captures in its hodgepodge nature both the high aspirations and the sordid realities of everyday life.

The Paradox of American Democracy

Whitman grappled with a central paradox: America strives to be great and powerful as a nation so that it can bring about the full flowering of individuals. "Political democracy, as it exists and practically works in America, with all its threatening evils, supplies a training school for making first-class men," he declared. "It is life's gymnasium, not of good only, but of all." Americans, he continued, are or should be "freedom's athletes," filled with "brave delight," audacious aims, and restless hopes.

Whitman longed for democratic noblemen and noblewomen who would be "in youth, fresh, ardent, emotional aspiring, full of adventure, at maturity, brave, perceptive, under control, neither too talkative nor too reticent, neither flippant nor somber, of the bodily figure, the movements easy, the complexion showing the best blood somewhat flushed, breast expanded, an erect attitude, a voice whose sound outvies music, eyes of calm and steady gaze, yet capable also of flashing." These people would realize themselves amid political combat, hard work, social reform, nation building, and global causes: "So will individuality, and unimpeded branchings, flourish best under imperial republican forms."

The forces of affluence, fashion, comfort, modesty, and civility were, Whitman feared, breeding "inertness and fossilism" in his countrymen and countrywomen. He embraced, as countermeasures, spirit and vivacity in every form, no matter how vulgar. "I hail with joy the oceanic, variegated, intense practical energy, the demand for facts, even the business materialism of the current age," he wrote. And he harbored the fervent hope that in the decades and centuries to come these raw energies would fuel spiritual and intellectual breakthroughs to create largeness of soul. "Thus we presume to write, as it were, upon things that exist not, and travel by maps yet unmade, and a blank. But the throes of birth are upon us."

Optimism in the Face of Bleakness

A cosmic optimism pervades the essay, as it does all of Whitman's works. But "Democratic Vistas" was actually written in a mood of some bleakness. Whitman had believed that the Civil War would cleanse the nation of its most serious ills. As the war approached and then commenced, he railed against business interests and war opponents—and and wrote several recruiting poems ("Thunder on! stride on, Democracy! strike with vengeful stroke!"). During the conflict he nursed the wounded. Literary critics sometimes emphasize the homoerotic nature of his attraction to the soldiers, but there was more to it than that. He admired their selfless heroism and their calmness and bravery as death approached. "Grand, common stock!" he exulted in "Democratic Vistas."

Whitman worked as a government clerk during the war, climbing from post to post, admiring [General Ulysses S.] Grant and worshipping [Abraham] Lincoln. Like everyone else, he had his moments of despair. "Every once in a while I feel so horrified & disgusted," he wrote to his mother in 1863. "[The war] seems to me like a great slaughter-house & the men mutually butchering each other." But even in such a dark moment, he continued, "I feel how impossible it appears again, to retire from this contest, until we have carried our points."

After the Union victory and Lincoln's sacrificial death, Whitman hoped that grief would cement the people together and call forth each person's best self. But of course the heroic mood did not survive. Life sank back to its normal, sordid pattern. Political and business corruption were rampant. The middle classes returned to their trivial enjoyments.

In April of 1867 the prophetic British historian Thomas Carlyle published an essay called "Shooting Niagara—and After?" It was a vituperative attack on democracy, equality, and the liberation of the slaves. Where the common people rule, he argued, all culture is brought low, and life becomes mediocre and vulgar. Whitman took up his pen to defend democracy and the United States. But by the time he completed his reply, "Democratic Vistas," he had to admit that Carlyle was right on many points.

Vacillations and Inconsistencies

Whitman's essay contains vacillations [alternations between different opinions] that give it a head-spinning quality. One paragraph expresses revulsion over the people he saw around him.

> Never was there, perhaps, more hollowness at heart than at present, and here in the United States. Genuine belief seems to have left us ... The spectacle is appalling. We live in an atmosphere of hypocrisy throughout. The men believe not in the women, nor the women in the men. A scornful superciliousness rules in literature. The aim of all the *littérateurs* is to find something to make fun of. A lot of churches, sects, etc., the most dismal phantasms I know, usurp the name of religion. Conversation is a mass of badinage [banter].

The next paragraph recounts his walking the streets of New York, amid the "assemblages of the citizens in their groups, conversations, trades and evening amusements," and finding himself overcome by "exaltation" and "absolute fulfillment." In the paragraph after that he is despondent again, unable to find around him men worthy of the name, or arts worthy of appreciation. "A sort of dry and flat Sahara appears, these cities, crowded with petty grotesques, malformations, phantoms, playing meaningless antics."

Whitman was teaching an important lesson here: It is misleading to think one can arrive at a single, consistent judgment about the United States (or perhaps about any society). When it comes to the health of the country and its culture, the highest highs and the lowest lows are simultaneous and adjacent. Extremes must be accepted without regard for consistency—a lesson that our gloomy cultural critics and self-congratulatory political orators almost never get right.

Optimism for the Future

In spite of his concessions to Carlyle, Whitman never fully reclined into pessimism. In the first place, his boundless energy always propelled him toward hopefulness, toward some activity that would lead to a brighter future. Second, unlike most cultural critics, he was not a snob, putting himself above those whose spiritual flatness he criticized. His love for his fellow Americans, as they actually lived and breathed around him, prevailed. No matter how trivial his neighbors might appear on the surface, he always saw through to their underlying nobility. "Shams, etc., will always be the show, like ocean's scum," he acknowledged. Even so, the American people were "the peaceablest and most good natured race in the world, and the most personally independent and intelligent." They were reliable in emergencies and possessed "a certain breadth of historic grandeur, of peace or war," in that regard surpassing the citizenry of any other great nation. The behavior of the average American during the Civil War, he contended, proved beyond all doubt "that popular democracy, whatever its faults and dangers, practically justifies itself beyond the proudest claims and wildest hopes of its enthusiasts." No future age could entirely know how the unknown rank and file of both armies fought and sacrificed for their ideals and proved themselves through "fearful tests."

Whitman had a remarkably subtle sense of America's unique historical mission. Many people before and since have argued that the United States was assigned by God or destiny to spread democracy and advance human freedom around the globe. But Whitman learned, perhaps from Lincoln, that this is both a glorious and a tragic assignment. Reading "Democratic Vistas" is a bit like looking at a painting of the Annunciation [of the birth of Jesus], as Mary glimpses the divine but sad future of her son.

Whitman foresaw that the country's task of promoting liberty and democracy would be an arduous one. He further foresaw that we would have to embrace that task even at times when life at home was far from perfect. America's mission would not always be a romantic quest headed by dashing, heroic figures. It would sometimes be led by Presidents (and others) who failed to be impressive or inspirational. "Even today, amid these whirls, incredible flippancy, and blind fury of parties, infidelity, entire lack of first-class captains and leaders," the United States is still destined to sail the "dangerous sea," he argued. He wrote,

> It seems as if the Almighty had spread before this nation charts of imperial destinies, dazzling as the sun, yet with many a deep intestine difficulty, and human aggregate of cankerous imperfection ... You said in your soul, I will be empire of empires, overshadowing all else, past and present, putting the history of Old-World dynasties, conquests behind me, as of no account—making a new history, a history of democracy, making old history a dwarf—I alone inaugurating largeness, culminating time.

A Powerful Rebuttal

Whitman also perceived that the nation could not readily communicate its mission, either to the world or to itself. He dreamed that a crop of literary giants would emerge to develop an American soul equal to American economic and political might. "Democratic Vistas" was intended to inspire a "literatus of the modern"—poets and writers who would complete the task Whitman had begun.

It's hard these days to put that much faith in poets and writers. The geniuses Whitman envisioned have not arrived. America's greatest contributions to the world are generally found in its innovations and its actions, not in literary masterpieces. Now, more than 130 years after Whitman published "Democratic Vistas," that essay remains the best explanation of the nation's energy and aspirations.

No one since Whitman has captured quite so well the motivating hopefulness that propels American policy and makes the nation a great and restless force in the world. No other essay communicates quite so well what it is like to live constantly in the shadow of the future, trusting that tomorrow's world will be better and will redeem the incompleteness of the present. Whitman's essay, with its nuanced understanding of the American national character, stands today as a powerful rebuttal to, for example, the parades of European anti-Americans. What these groups despise is a cliché—a flat and simpleminded image of American power. They do not see, as Whitman did, that despite its many imperfections, America is a force for democracy and progress. "Far, far indeed, stretch, in distance, our Vistas!" Whitman wrote. "How much is still to be disentangled, freed!"

Whitman Offers a Complex, Imaginative Model of Patriotism

Stephen Cushman

Stephen Cushman is Robert C. Taylor Professor of English, specializing in American literature and poetry, at the University of Virginia.

Cushman argues in the following viewpoint that, although Walt Whitman's patriotism might appear quaint to the casual observer, in fact it was a matter of great seriousness to the poet. He formed his ideas in a time of upheaval unparalleled in American history, and his apparent swaggering was actually a response to malignant forces that threatened the very fabric of the still-young republic. Yet Whitman did not speak explicitly of patriotism, eschewing abstract symbolism in favor of a more heartfelt celebration of the country he loved. Even, or perhaps especially, in the wake of the September 2001 terrorist attacks, Cushman says, Whitman offers a model for a thoughtful, critical patriotism that encourages Americans to think more broadly about the country and its place in the world.

"The United States themselves are essentially the greatest poem." What presidential speechwriter, talk-radio host, bumper-sticker sloganeer, or all-around flag-waver has ever written or spoken higher praise? What anthem or pledge, sung or recited before a sports event or at a school, contains so unabashed a superlative? This simple declarative sentence, the second one of the second paragraph on the first page of the first edition of *Leaves of Grass*, approaches its 150th birthday

Stephen Cushman, "Whitman and Patriotism," *Virginia Quarterly Review*, vol. 81, no. 2, 2005, pp. 163–77. All rights reserved. Reproduced by permission.

still strutting its uncompromising, unqualified assertiveness. True, one could argue that "essentially" implies a slight hedge, as it does in the statement "With only minutes to go, this lop-sided game is essentially over," where "essentially" means "just about" or "pretty much" or "for all practical purposes," and one could look to the first sentence of the same paragraph, with its "probably," for support of such an argument: "The Americans of all nations at any time upon the earth have probably the fullest poetical nature."

But as the rest of the second paragraph suggests, Whitman really is talking about essence here, about something inherent and fundamental: "Here at last is something in the doings of man that corresponds with the broadcast doings of the day and night. Here is not merely a nation but a teeming nation of nations. Here is action untied from strings necessarily blind to particulars and details magnificently moving in vast masses." Particulars and details "magnificently moving in vast masses," a phrase with all the auditory repetitions and palpabilities of Whitman's language in verse, are particulars and details that start from discrete separateness and converge to point to the comprehensive and general, to the commonly shared and essential.

What some might call Whitman's essentialism is only one of the features of his statement about the United States that might mark it, in some eyes, as dated, obsolete, historically confined and limited. Another is his use of the plural verb "are," as opposed to the "is" that gradually became dominant after the American Civil War forever rearranged the notion of an American nation. Only 79 years into the American experiment in 1855, Whitman's grammar reflects the evolving balance between, on the one hand, the *plura* of *e pluribus* and, on the other, the emerging *unum* under construction. In addition, without listening closely to history, or to various histories, we might not catch the note of desperate, even doomed, hopefulness behind the vatic [prophetic] pronouncement that the United States are essentially the greatest poem. With the passage of the Kansas-Nebraska Act [1854 act of Congress allowing citizens of Kansas and Nebraska to decide by vote whether slavery would be permitted in those territories] the year before and the first virulent eruptions of the killing that would go on for more than a decade, Whitman is not so much swaggering and flexing as he is urgently speaking a spell or charm against social and political malignancy, even as it too rapidly metastasizes.

Whitman's Patriotism

To some Whitman's assertion may sound too grandiose and embarrassing, to others too airy and vague, but rather than spend more time attempting to interpret or defend or redeem the statement in all its slippery figurativeness (what does he mean by a metaphor that compares a country to a poem?), I want to turn instead to the larger issue of Whitman's patriotism. In doing so, I have two goals in mind. First, I want to confront that patriotism in different forms and phases in order to appraise Whitman's management of celebration and criticism at a few selected moments in his life and writing. Second, I want to use that appraisal to ground some thinking about Whitman as a possible model for combining celebration and criticism of the United States 150 years after the first appearance of *Leaves of Grass*. Although we hear the words "patriot," "patriotic," and "patriotism" all around us—Patriots' Day (there are two, actually), Patriot Act, Patriot missile, New England Patriots come to mind—we do not have many useful public models for combining genuine celebration of the United States with constructive criticism of it. Perhaps the divisions of left and right have made such a combination impossible. Perhaps various kinds of pressure, refracted through print and visual media, leave most people feeling that they can either celebrate or criticize but not do both. I earnestly hope not, and in trying to affirm one or more productive alternatives to monotonal praise or blame, I want to consider whether or not Whitman's example still can help.

If Whitman thought of himself as a patriot or as patriotic, he did not say so explicitly in the writings he published. In fact, "patriot" and its cognate [having the same root] forms rarely appear in his two major books, *Leaves of Grass* (9th edition, 1891–92) and *Complete Prose Works* (1892). According to Edwin Harold Eby's 1949 concordance to *Leaves of Grass* and selected prose writings, Whitman uses "patriot" in only two poems, "patriots'" in one, and "patriotism" in only one place in Eby's selection of his prose. Even more interesting than the scarcity of appearances, though, is their chronology. Three of the four appear in Whitman's later writing, published after his voluntary service in Washington military hospitals during the Civil War and after what is probably the most famous use of "patriot" in 19th-century American letters, its appearance in the final, syntactically complex and rhythmically triumphant sentence of Lincoln's first inaugural address, delivered March 4, 1861: "The mystic chords of memory, stretching from every battle-field, and patriot grave, to every living heart and hearth-stone, all over this broad land, will yet swell the chorus of the Union, when again touched, as surely they will be, by the better angels of our nature." . . .

Different readers might offer different explanations for the paucity [scarcity] of direct; references to patriotism in Whitman's writing, but one that feels plausible to me is that someone so deeply engaged in celebrating various aspects of the United States, and in identifying himself with his image or images of an American ethos, had little need or ability to separate himself from that celebration and objectify it with an abstract term like "patriotism." Or, to put the matter more bluntly and reductively, Whitman was too busy celebrating himself and his country, and insisting on the connections between them, to spend much time crowing self-righteously about how patriotic he was and how deeply he believed in the value of patriotism. . . .

Walt Whitman, American

[W]e can [now] move to one of the most famous moments in the untitled poem of 1855 that eventually became "Song of Myself," the moment of self-naming and self-annunciation: "Walt Whitman, an American, one of the roughs, a kosmos." As many readers have noticed and commented, this line, the 499th of a 1,336-line poem in 1855, marks the first appearance of the name "Walt Whitman" in the first edition of *Leave of Grass.* Whitman having deliberately omitted it from the title page, which faces the notoriously iconic, knee-length image of him with cocked hat, open shirt collar, right fist on right hip, and left hand in left pocket. Turning the title page, one finds, as the curious [Ralph Waldo] Emerson did, that "Walter Whitman" entered the copyright for the book, but the usual authorial conventions of making a name for oneself have been nonchalantly ignored, not out of humility—hardly so in Whitman's case—but out of a strategy to tease and seduce the readerly "you" addressed most directly and extensively in "Song of Myself."

What fewer readers have noticed is that this line also contains the first use of "American," or any cognate of "America," in the poems of the 1855 *Leaves of Grass* (those cognates do appear several times in the preface), and I want to linger for a moment over the triad of nouns Whitman uses to identify and introduce himself before he passes quickly on to a series of self-descriptive adjectives and participles, also arranged in two sets of triads: "Disorderly fleshy and sensual . . . eating drinking and breeding." For all the confident bravado sounded in this introduction, which he has coyly deferred for more than a third of his poem, subsequent revisions show plenty of second thoughts and second-guessing about the best way to identify himself. Through the first three editions of *Leaves of Grass,* 1855, 1856, and 1860, the line stays the same, but in the fourth (1867) edition, the first after the end of the Civil War, the line reads, a little too grandiloquently [pompously] for my ear, "Walt Whitman am I, of mighty Manhattan the son," before taking its final form in 1871: "Walt Whitman, a kosmos, of Manhattan the son."

What may feel to some like a very small textual molehill in fact speaks mountains' worth about Whitman's sense of patriotism....

Modeling Whitman's Patriotism

In September 2001 our older son began his freshman year at a local public high school. Soon after the attacks that month he brought home from the school a list of ten virtues or moral qualities the school has chosen to try to develop in its students, and he asked us to guess the virtue ranked first. Compassion? Truthfulness? Responsibility? Cooperativeness? Integrity? One of the four Platonic virtues, wisdom, courage, temperance, justice? Faith, hope, charity, the three added by Christianity to make the seven cardinal virtues and offset the seven deadly sins? Wrong, wrong, wrong, all wrong. When he revealed the answer to be patriotism, he also revealed his own uncertainty about the meaning and implication of such a ranking. What could Whitman say to him? Believer in the destiny of the United States to expand into Canada and the Caribbean; champion of white labor and underestimator of the egalitarian humanities informing other strains of abolitionism; sufferer of acute alienation from the conventions and comforts of mid-19th-century American sexual mores; self-promoting opportunist determined to perform the role of national bard at the cost of suppressing other images of himself: what could such a person tell him about patriotism in the United States in the first decade of the 21st century?

If nothing else, that it is, or can be, profoundly complicated and difficult in often bewildering ways, which the shorthand term "ambivalence" cannot cover and the wearing of an American flag pin on a lapel cannot foreclose. Our son might look to Whitman in the context of patriotism not because he should believe for a moment that Whitman's example gives him any easy answers or formulae to brandish in moments of doubt and confusion, but because Whitman wrote so much and, often, so well about his own struggles to understand himself in relation to the United States, its strengths and its weaknesses, although he himself would not necessarily have acknowledged that struggle. Is he the only writer to whom one could turn in this context? Certainly not. But since his struggles with a sense of national identity and its limits unfolded against a period before, during, and after a war, though admittedly a war unlike any other in which American soldiers have fought and died before or since, many might feel a consideration of his case is more timely than those of others we could name.

For one thing, Whitman showed that the support of soldiers fighting a war—and in his case this support entailed exhausting practical services—did not preclude stringent criticism of those in charge of those soldiers. Although we cannot know for sure whether a 21st-century Whitman would have opted for a bumper sticker urging others to support the troops, it is doubtful he would have endorsed any implicit subtext of such a bumper sticker, if he felt that subtext pointing to the prohibition of questioning and criticizing the people responsible for the lives of those troops. In *Memoranda During the War*, for example, after the Union disaster at First Manassas/Bull Run (July 1861), he unleashes on the officers, presumably the general or field ones most likely to be frequenting Willard's Hotel [a Washington, DC, lodging establishment favored by visiting dignitaries], this barrage: "There you are, shoulder-straps!—but where are your companies? where are your men? Incompetents! never tell me of chances of battle, of getting strayed, and the like. I think this is your work, this retreat, after all. Sneak, blow, put on airs there in Willard's sumptuous parlors and bar-rooms, or anywhere—no explanation shall save you. Bull Run is your work; had you been half or one-tenth worthy your men, this would never have happen'd." Whitman hardly had a monopoly on this kind of criticism, since disasters in war often lead to fault-finding and finger-pointing among both military and civilian populations, as readers of wartime newspapers can attest. But the preservation of such a passage in a published work confirms Whitman's resistance to any notion of patriotism as necessarily silencing objections to the conduct of war.

A Critical, Questioning Patriotism

Whitman could also help someone prone to reductive oversimplification, whether a high school student or a fully enfranchised voter, see that there is no necessary incompatibility between celebrating what he thought of and described as the American average, on the one hand, and criticizing American politicians and officeholders, on the other. Likewise, as several passages from *Democratic Vistas* make clear, Whitman could help someone think more critically about what lies behind the conveniently lazy phrase "The American Way of Life," and particularly about exhortations to defend it, by demonstrating that there is no necessary incompatibility between the affirmation of American democracy, especially in theory, and the deploring of the excesses and distortions of American capitalism in actual practice, whether in the 19th or the 21st century.

Although *Democratic Vistas* reflects Whitman's postwar anxieties about that capitalism, his worries about the soullessness of American money-worship also inform the first edition of *Leaves of Grass*. Published the year after [American political philosopher Henry David Thoreau's] *Walden* (1854), one long, undulating sentence from Whitman's first preface, only partly quoted here, reflects many of the challenges to American economic imperatives that Thoreau launched in his opening chapter, "Economy": "Beyond the independence of a little sum laid aside for burial-money, and of a few clapboards around and shingles overhead on a lot of American soil owned, and the easy dollars that supply the year's plain clothing and meals, the melancholy prudence of the abandonment of such a great being as a man is to the toss and pallor of years of money-making with all their scorching days and icy nights and all their stifling deceits and underhanded dodgings, or infinitessimals of parlors, or shameless stuffing while others starve . . . is the great fraud upon modern civilization. . . ." In Whitman's image of "melancholy prudence" we may hear an echo of Thoreau's famous dictum, "The mass of men lead lives of quiet desperation." This comparison is particularly instructive, since it allows us to see ways in which Thoreau and Whitman also diverge, the former indicting the pernicious effects of American economic compulsions while also separating himself from the mass of men and their government, as is especially evident in "Resistance to Civil Government" (1849; later "Civil Disobedience"), whereas the latter indicts those compulsions at the same time that he still thinks of himself as actively engaged with or connected to American politics and government.

Finally, Whitman's patriotism, inconsistent, fluctuating, self-interested, self-forgetful as it was by turns, could show a high school freshman or anyone else that patriotism need not and should not keep one from making imaginative cosmopolitan connections with people in other countries. . . . For Whitman these connections were neither superficial nor facile, and even though they remained imaginary for him, as do many of our own connections with people beyond the borders that define our citizenship, they also carried with them a deep, troubling identification with others throughout the world, an identification without which no one's patriotism, not a student's, not a poet's, not a president's, can hope to free itself from narcissism chained to a national mirror.

A Twenty-First-Century Whitman Would Express His Views Through Rock and Roll

David Haven Blake

David Haven Blake is a professor of English at the College of New Jersey and the author of Walt Whitman and the Culture of American Celebrity.

In the following essay, Blake imagines Walt Whitman's role in American society if he were alive in the twenty-first century. Blake envisions Whitman not as a poet and professor of literature but rather as a rock-and-roll lyricist. Musical performance, especially in the aggressively intimate and often seedy environment of rock-and-roll venues, would provide Whitman with the kind of interactive relationship with his followers that he considered necessary to the understanding of his work. Rock music, Blake argues, is more heart than art, and Whitman made a similar distinction between the poetry and music of the Old World versus that of the New World. According to Blake, the emergence of poetry slams—high-energy poetry competitions that emphasize crowd interaction—in recent decades proves the correlation between poetry and rock and roll.

On the 150th anniversary of *Leaves of Grass*, I have a confession to make: I wonder whether Whitman would be a poet in the 21st century. I try to picture him in an MFA [master of fine arts degree program] classroom, his salutations and self-reference left on the workshop floor, and I invariably conclude that if he were alive today, old Walt would be playing rock 'n' roll. Whether as a solitary singer or the leader of a

David Haven Blake, "Reading Whitman, Growing Up Rock 'n' Roll," *Virginia Quarterly Review*, vol. 81, no. 2, Spring 2005, pp. 34–47. All rights reserved. Reproduced by permission.

band, he'd wish to command the stage with the same sweaty genius as the guitar heroes who now inhabit the persona he created many years ago. For a poet who dreamed of pressing close to his audience and possessing their very best, rock 'n' roll would have been a natural and satisfying cultural development. "I was chilled with the cold types and cylinder and wet paper between us," Whitman told his readers in 1855; "I pass so poorly with the paper and types. . . . I must pass with the contact of bodies." More than any of its aesthetic counterparts, rock revels in the kind of intimate, bodily sympathy Whitman envisioned between his audience and himself, and perhaps only rock has made that vision a tangible, public reality. . . .

Rock Music Is Highly Personal

With the exception of television, no cultural influence in the last forty years has been as powerful and pervasive as popular music. Across a startling range of forms and styles—heavy metal, hip-hop, emo, rhythm and blues, glam, jam, grunge, and punk (to name just a few)—the music has shaped everything from our fantasies to our sexuality to the way we express emotional conflict. (How much rage has been sublimated through the recordings of the Who, the Sex Pistols, and Tupac Shakur?) This is especially true for young people whose choice of music has traditionally conveyed not just fleeting emotions but deep personal values. From the Vietnam War to the struggle against apartheid, rock has proven to be an especially good agent for raising social consciousness because it is so effective in altering its listeners' conceptions of self. With unstudied brilliance, it replicates the promise, quite familiar to readers of Whitman and [his contemporary, philosopher/essayist Ralph Waldo] Emerson, that artists will bring about an awakening in the audience, that their public works will take on a highly personal significance. "A great poem," Whitman wrote in 1855, "is no finish to a man or woman but rather a beginning." More than any of its cultural competitors—television programs, films, paintings, sculpture, symphonies, plays, and books—rock has become the predominant cultural setting for the testing and assertion of identity. Young men and women approach their music with the ardent seriousness of play, selecting each recording as if it conveyed something ineffable about themselves. In his famous "Calamus" cluster, Whitman suggested that he had left "faint clews and indirections" for his readers, hoping that their interest in his mysterious personality would result in a reformation of their own. Roughly one hundred years later, rock 'n' roll emerged, and within a decade, its fans were studying album covers and parsing lyrics in a remarkable conflation of self-discovery and hero worship.

It is of course customary to speak of rock's most talented lyricists as poets—so effective their lyrics are in capturing a wide range of emotional experience. And there are plenty of songwriters whom critics have described as literary because their songs reveal a familiarity with the world of books. The problem with the label "rock poet" is that it suggests that the music needs to be dressed up in order to be taken seriously; poetry becomes a kind of fancy pants affixed to the naked loins of rock 'n' roll. Whitman would have had little interest in the term, for particularly in the first decade of his career, he was disinclined to view his poems as a culturally authoritative art. The preface to the 1855 edition of *Leaves of Grass* makes clear that poetry comes not from the parlor but from the street. It tells readers that they must "stand up for the stupid and crazy," that they must "go freely with powerful uneducated persons and with the young and with the mothers of families" if their bodies are to become poems themselves. Poetry comes not from the library, not from universities, but from the public association of stevedores, mechanics, prostitutes, and runaway slaves. Rather than a music that pretended

Photograph of rock and roll legend Chuck Berry at Sunset Lake Park in Portsmouth, Virginia, in 1959. Over half a century later, when Chuck Berry was awarded the first PEN New England Song Lyrics of Literary Excellence Award, his co-recipient, Leonard Cohen, said that Berry's song "Roll Over Beethoven" was the rock and roll incarnation of Walt Whitman's joyful noise. © Historical/Bettmann/Corbis.

to be poetry, Whitman would want a poetry informed by the music of workers singing about themselves.

Art-Singing vs. Heart-Singing

Writing in the *Broadway Journal* in 1845, Whitman distinguished between art-singing and heart-singing, the former associated with European performers and the latter with those from the United States. European music, he wrote, was "made to please royal ears," and in that respect, it had adequately expressed the character of aristocratic society. Despite the popularity of "the tenors, boffos, and operatic troupes" who toured in the New World, Whitman had detected the emergence of an American strain of music, a music that appealed "to the throbbings of the great heart of humanity itself." In groups such as the Hutchinson and Cheney families, he heard the unadorned, original beauty of the human voice. Commenting on the Cheneys' performance at a New York saloon, he praised the "elegant simplicity" of the family's style: "Thus, said we in our heart, is the true method which must become popular in the United States—which must supplant the stale, second-hand, foreign method, with its flourishes, its ridiculous sentimentality, its anti-republican spirit, and its sycophantic influence, tainting the young taste of the republic." In the heart-singing of Americans, Whitman found a native-born simplicity that by expressing the soul of democracy, expressed the soul of humanity as well.

In making a distinction between art music and heart music, in emphasizing the importance of simplicity and the soul, Whitman was on the road towards making a broader statement about what constituted aesthetic value. By the end of the 1840s, he had become an ardent fan of opera, a dignified, but still popular entertainment that was just beginning to take on its current aristocratic associations. The poet's love of the opera is legendary. In "Song of Myself," he describes hearing a soprano and convulsing as if he had climaxed, the music placing him amid "the steeps of honeyed morphine." His own aria-like laments in "Out of the Cradle Endlessly Rocking" affirm that despite his early misgivings, he found tremendous aesthetic possibility in European singing. "A new world—a liquid worlds—rushes like a torrent through you," Whitman wrote after a performance of [Giuseppe] Verdi's [opera] *Ernani*. "If you have the true musical feeling in you, from this night you date a new era in your development, and, for the first time, receive your ideas of what the divine art of music really is."

While Whitman's appreciation for European composers evolved over time, he retained his belief that heart music would be the foundation of American song. When he heard America singing, he heard the voices of individuals rather than of traditions or schools. The songs Americans sang were intimately tied to their identity—not as artists but as laborers:

I hear America singing, the varied carols I
hear,

Those of mechanics, each one singing his as
it should be blithe and strong,

The carpenter singing his as he measures his
plank or beam,

The mason singing his as he makes ready
for work, or leaves off work,

The boatman singing what belongs to him
in his boat, the deckhand singing on the
steamboat deck,

The shoemaker singing as he sits on his
bench, the hatter singing as he stands,

The wood-cutter's song, the ploughboy's on
his way in the morning, or at noon intermission or at sundown,

The delicious singing of the mother, or of
the young wife at work, or of the girl sewing
or washing,

Each singing what belongs to him or her
and to none else,

The day what belongs to the day—at night
the party of young fellows, robust, friendly,

Singing with open mouths their strong me-
lodious songs.

To Whitman, the voices of American singers conveyed history,
experience, and work; their songs arose not from their aesthetic genius but from their individual character. We cannot
expect these voices to have been conventionally beautiful or
artistic. The voices Whitman heard were strained, cracked,
heavily accented, and perhaps even out of tune. But it was out
of this music, this democratic heart-singing, that "the party of
young fellows" emerged, singing their songs into the night,
their voices robust and strong.

Whitman and African-American Music

Although he coined the phrase ten years before the publication of *Leaves of Grass*, Whitman's interest in heart-singing
would remain with him until the end of his life. He several
times stated that the most fertile ground for cultivating a distinctly American music was the African-American experience.
In *An American Primer*, he praised the regenerative power of
black English, arguing that the speech of slaves had "hints of
the future theory of the modification of all the words of the
English language, for musical purposes, for a native grand opera in America, leaving the words just as they are for writing
and speaking, but the same words so modified as to answer
perfectly for musical purposes, on grand and simple principles." When Horace Traubel asked him about American music in 1889, the poet pointed to the songs that came out of the

South. America's "best work so far" seemed to be in the direction of slave songs. Songs such as "Old Folks at Home" and "Old Black Joe" were superb, Whitman said, "exquisite specimens, some of them, out of the heart of nature—hitting off" Southern life with "wonderful expression."

Whitman did not attribute these songs to Stephen Foster, the white composer who wrote and arranged them. As he described them, the songs came from a culture, not an individual. The racist quality of Foster's songs is glaringly apparent today, a fact punctuated by Whitman's repeated description of them as "nigger songs." And yet, like W.E.B. DuBois, the poet seemed to hear in such songs a promising engagement with African-American music, the "whole phrases of Negro melody," as DuBois put it in *The Souls of Black Folk*, giving structure to Foster's compositions. W.C. Handy would later come to a similar conclusion, commenting in his autobiography, *Father of the Blues*, songs such as "My Old Kentucky Home" owed their existence to the same "well of sorrow from which Negro music is drawn." It is hard to imagine a music more immersed in heart-singing than the songs that arose from the violence, prejudice, and poverty of the South. What Whitman heard in the background of Foster's melodies were the songs that [former slave and abolitionist] Frederick Douglass credited with awakening his own understanding of slavery, the sorrow songs that would eventually lead to gospel, ragtime, jazz, and the blues. As [Whitman scholar] Larry Griffin points out in his contribution to *Utopia in the Present Tense*, Whitman's "native grand opera" emerged out of the African-American experience and animated the nation at large. It would later surface in the many variants and descendants of rock 'n' roll. . . .

Whitman Would Have Appreciated Rock

As we mark the sesquicentennial of the 1855 *Leaves of Grass*, poetry may be gravitating towards the energy and ritualism of rock. Rock music has changed what many readers and writers expect from the literary world, and Whitman would have been pleased at the initial results. Late in life, he mourned his inability to travel to different cities and promote his book, wanting to "whack about" and "bargain" himself in New York, Chicago, and St. Louis. The profusion of readings today follows Whitman's notion that the performance of a charismatic personality is vital to the success of American poetry. Some of the poets most identified with *Leaves of Grass*—Allen Ginsberg, Anne Sexton, and Sherman Alexie—have not only been interested in live performance; they have also lent their talents to rock 'n' roll. The rise of the poetry slam may signal the emergence of a refreshingly hybrid literary form. With its emphasis on affect, competition, and the crowd's response, the slam has invigorated the culture of poetry with the Dionysian [spontaneous and sensual] energy of a rock show. In coming years, it will be interesting to see whether the traditional university reading begins to incorporate the openness and immediacy that audiences value in slam competitions throughout the United States.

"What always indicates the poet," Whitman wrote, "is the crowd of the pleasant company of singers, and their words." Listeners have found in rock the sense of inspired self-empowerment that Whitman hoped Americans would get from his poems. Far outside fantasies of fame and wealth, people identify with the music. They buy instruments and teach themselves how to play. They form garage bands; they play middle school dances; they drum on plastic tubs outside the subway. Across the globe, the music has created a multitude of singers and musicians who have defined its traditions anew. Rock's capacity to engage the listener as a participant eradicates the old creative boundaries between artists and the people who stood humbled by their work. The turntable was once an appliance for delivering someone else's songs. Thanks to some innovative teenagers in the Bronx, it is now widely recognized as an instrument.

In the same spirit, we can read *Leaves of Grass* for the poet's sweeping and sonorous voice, marveling at the poems as they descend to us from years ago; or, we can accept the challenge of joining the pleasant company of singers who find their music in his words. These options reveal Whitman's promise rather than a delimiting choice. "I am with you, you men and women of a generation, or ever so many generations hence," he proclaims in "Crossing Brooklyn Ferry," confident that we will turn to him as a source of comfort, nourishment, and health. "What thoughts you have of me now, I had as much of you—I laid in my stores in advance." Perhaps anticipating anniversaries such as this one, he knew that in reimagining his work, we would reimagine ourselves.

Whitman Loved America with a Ferocity Tempered by Compassion

C.K. Williams

C.K. Williams is a poet and the author of the study On Whitman.

Even though Walt Whitman frequently chastised America and its leaders for their inability to recognize the highest good in themselves and others, he was first and foremost an American patriot. In the following essay, C.K. Williams describes Whitman's love of American democracy and his belief that his poetry could be used as a tool to help Americans identify and live up to their ideals. Whitman is shown to have made very deliberate formal and linguistic choices to infuse Leaves of Grass *(1855) with his sense of Americanness. Even in his most abstract and mystical poems, Whitman reaches such heights through his use of distinctly American language, imagery, and thought.*

How [Whitman] loves America in that first preface to *Leaves of Grass*. Like a schoolboy, like a youth in an unquestioning patriotic frenzy. How ragingly later on, before and during the Civil War, he would curse the "disunionists" who dared sunder the nation, sunder his hopes for its greatness. And how he loves democracy. The vision he has for democracy, his hopes for America, are almost painful to bring to mind. How short we have fallen compared to what he saw for us, how in so many ways have we regressed.

Whitman wants his poem to be democracy embodied, enacted; he wants to omit nothing. Democracy at its essence is

C.K. Williams, "America," in *On Whitman*. Princeton, NJ: Princeton University Press, 2010, pp. 65–74. All rights reserved. Reproduced by permission.

the detail, not the generalization, or at least the detail first, then the generalization; the "I," because we have to begin there, and the "we," and then the "you," and there, in essence, the equation is done—there is, as he points out again and again, no "they": "they" is the thought of the crowd, the mob, the mockers. Even during the Civil War, however nearly obsessed he was about preserving the Union, the being-together, the Confederate warriors are still a portion of "we," his compassion never flags, no matter who is firing the weapon, who receiving the wound.

Poetry and America's Destiny

He really meant all that rhetoric in the first preface; he really did want his poetry to help, or compel what he thought America could be, had to be. He really believed his poetry was an efficient implement for creating the America of his vision. Although first he wanted to enable Americans to be sufficient to that nation—he believed his words would signify and seduce them from their incomplete awareness of the task—Americans who would then construct the America he knew was latent, and necessary, for the country's future. He happily confounds (and only in retrospect absurdly conflates) the future of the country with his vision of the poet who will embody it. "Of all nations the United States with veins full of poetical stuff most need poets and will doubtless have the greatest and use them the greatest. Their Presidents shall not be their common referee so much as their poets shall."

Later, after he's written the great poems, he states, in *Democratic Vistas*, just as passionately the connection he believes there must exist between his work and his country's destiny:

> I say no land or people or circumstances ever existed so needing a race of singers and poems differing from all others, and rigidly their own, as the land and people and circumstances of our United States need such singers and po-

157

ems today, and for the future. . . . As long as the States continue to absorb and be dominated by the poetry of the Old World, and remain unsupplied with autochthonous [native] song, to express, vitalize and give color to and define their material and political success, and minister to them distinctively, so long will they stop short of first-class Nationality and remain defective.

His hopes for us were limitless; he even postulated, in the poems and in *Democratic Vistas*, a certain physique for the American, a certain degree of health. He often, too often perhaps, speaks of "health," in various manifestations; he loves the word itself and finds dozens of ways of indicating it in the body and mind, and even in institutions: "These American states strong and healthy and accomplished shall receive no pleasure from violations of natural models." (Sad, considering how young he was when his own body began to turn against him with a series of strokes, the first at the terribly early age of fifty-four, then later, in the various disabilities of aging.)

Interestingly, he's aesthetically very conscious, cunning, about the best way to embody his patriotism. In the first edition of *Leaves*, after going on at such great length about America in the preface, he's a good long way into the poem before the word ever appears, and it does so then in the introduction of the author . . . : "Walt Whitman, an American, one of the roughs, a kosmos." And further, though he invokes the battle of Goliad in the Mexican War; then a famous American sea battle, and the names of several states and cities (including Montreal), the word never again appears in that first version of the poem. Not until the 1860 edition does the word make its rather theatrical appearance in "I Hear America Singing," which, with its compilation of a long list of hardworking tradesmen and honest mothers and wives, sounds now like the progenitor of a hundred Broadway and Hollywood fauxproletariat musicals.

Walt Whitman praises New York City's energetic exuberance in this quotation from "City of Ships," one of the poems in his Leaves of Grass *collection. The quotation was inscribed in 1986 on this Battery Park City railing, at the southern tip of Manhattan, overlooking the Hudson River and Jersey City, New Jersey. (Photograph taken in March 2008.)* © Terese Loeb Kreuzer/Alamy.

An Aesthetic, Spiritual America

His not using the word "America," though, is more effective than not and honors his task more clearly: rather than refer directly to America, he makes his poem embody the nation at its best. He aestheticizes and spiritualizes America and its people; and he tells what a fully conscious American would see and feel if he could share Whitman's genius, and the poem does, of course, allow us to partake of that genius. The hundreds of American characters who populate and ennoble the poem, the dozens of anecdotes of their strength, their integrity, their distinctness—even when they lag, when they're part of a crowd, for instance, who are ridiculing a prostitute—he appeals to their native goodness, their compassion, their sympathy—"*Miserable! I do not laugh at your oaths or jeer you.*"

Still, Whitman was no dreamer, no rose-lensed optimist, no self-deluder: he proves himself in the prose painfully aware

159

of America's greater faults, its incompleteness, its derelictions, its corruptions and crassness and despicable failures. In *Democratic Vistas*, he all but rants, as though tragically disappointed in his country: "Never was there, perhaps, more hollowness at heart than at present, and here in the United States. . . . What penetrating eye does not everywhere see through the mask? . . . We live in an atmosphere of hypocrisy throughout. . . . The depravity of the business classes of our country is not less than has been supposed, but infinitely greater. The official services of America, national, state, and municipal, in all their branches and departments, except the judiciary, are saturated in corruption, bribery, falsehood, mal-administrating; and the judiciary is tainted." He quotes a "foreigner," who reports similar gloomy observations, including one that strikes sadly home these days: "I have noticed more and more, the alarming spectacle of parties usurping the government, and openly and shamelessly wielding it for party purposes." (What we've come to now, politics by party, politics as power—doesn't that instruct us to mistrust, to loathe?) He already knew the loss, and almost with a cry against himself, though in his fervor of exaggeration he surely doesn't mean it, he laments, "America has yet morally and artistically originated nothing."

A Hymn of Praise to America

But of course it had, it had originated much, including *Leaves of Grass*, which is a hymn of praise to the nation, to its people, its land, its nature, its animals—"*When the mockingbird sounds his delicious gurgles, and cackles, and screams and weeps*"—and its cities, its rivers, and its "*gneiss and coal and long-threaded moss and fruits and grains and esculent roots.*" Even the lowest, the slaves, and slavery, which in the preface he castigates: "Slavery and the tremulous spreading of hands to protect it, and the stern opposition to it which shall never cease till it ceases or the speaking of tongues and the moving of lips cease." And in the poems, again and again he powerfully and poignantly castigates it:

> I am the hounded slave . . . I wince at the
> bite of the dogs,
>
> Hell and despair are upon me . . . crack and
> again crack the marksmen,
>
> I clutch the rails of the fence . . . my gore
> dribs thinned with the ooze of my skin,
>
> I fall on the weeds and stones,
>
> The riders spur their unwilling horses and
> haul close,
>
> They taunt my dizzy ears . . . they beat me
> violently over the head with their whip-
> stocks.

And even again, his body, which is an American body, a body born of all his accumulations, all his accountings for, and which is composed in his ecstatic vision of all the other bodies, and even of those bodies dying and already in death: Americans, America, all of it. And the soul, the spirit, all of it, even those who have lost faith in the soul and spirit:

> Down-hearted doubters, dull and excluded,
>
> Frivolous sullen moping angry affected dis-
> heartened atheistial,
>
> I know every one of you, and I know the
> unspoken interrogatories.
>
> By experience I know them.

Then, immediately from that, one of his wild poetic somersaults:

> How the flukes splash!

> How they contort rapid as lightning, with
> spasms and spouts of blood!

A symbolization that he resolves as only he can:

> Be at peace bloody flukes of doubters and
> sullen mopers,
>
> I take my place among you as much as
> among any . . .

And so his vision not only encompasses the enemy soldier, the fireman, the slave, the adulteress, it includes the thrush and ant and weed: it's not incidental that he reaches back to the year one, "sesquillions" of cycles behind us—democracy includes past and future because its vision generates both, in a way even religion is unable to, or dares not to.

> Cycles ferried my cradle, rowing and rowing
> like cheerful boatmen;
>
> For room to me stars kept aside in their
> own rings,
>
> They sent influences to look after what was
> to hold me.

Committed to an American Perspective

Even when he addresses the universe itself, and the metaphysical universe he devolves from it, though he never has to say so overtly, he is still American, still firmly committed to the perspective, the viewing place the rest of the poem has created to contain him; no matter how far into eternity he reaches, he is there in his language, his beloved American language, which, in this early manifestation of it, he never for an instant betrays, as he will sometimes later, with what at better moments he'd called "European" poeticisms, contractions, artifices. (In "An American Primer," a sketch he wrote but never published, he proclaims it even more insistently: "I think I am done with many of the words of the past hundred centuries.—I am mad that their poems, bibles, word, still rule and represent the earth, and are not yet superseded.") In the poems themselves, no matter how elevated his theme, how grand his physics and metaphysics, his language insisted on being that of actual Americans, of the streets they inhabited, the cities and landscapes he believed made them great.

Contemporary
Perspectives
on Democracy

Democracy Requires an Informed Electorate

Henry Aubin

Henry Aubin, a journalist for the Montreal Gazette, *is the author of* The Rescue of Jerusalem: The Alliance Between Hebrews and Africans in 701 B.C.

Participatory democracy is intended to create equality by placing equal value on the vote of each citizen. Voting, however, is not only a right but also a responsibility, argues Aubin in the following viewpoint. He states that voting without properly understanding the issues at hand and each candidate's stance in relation to them is dangerous and devalues the efforts of those who cast educated, thoughtful votes. Aubin attributes increasing political ignorance to the rise of extreme individualism and a declining sense of community, and he suggests that it would be preferable to have the uninformed abstain from voting.

Between now and Monday's [May 2, 2011,] federal election [in Canada] you will hear countless appeals to vote. Commentators, civic groups and campus organizations will make the same standard argument.

They'll remind you that soldiers died to ensure that you live in a democracy. They'll note that—as the demonstrators during this Arab Spring so vividly show—much of the world envies our democracy. And they'll conclude with the ringing maxim that the fundamental duty of every citizen in a democracy is to vote.

Everything in this argument is true—and worth honouring—except the maxim. It needs amending. The fundamental duty of every citizen in a democracy is to be informed and then—and only then—vote.

In this January 28, 2011, image of "Arab Spring" in Cairo, Egypt, activists demanding the immediate end of President Hosni Mubarak's thirty-year reign clash with riot police. Journalist Henry Aubin notes that scenes such as this one are used to urge voter participation in democratic countries where citizens enjoy the luxury of voting without violence. © AP Images/Ben Curtis.

The idea that there is some virtue in hurling oneself at a polling station and simply voting for the sake of voting is nonsense. Better for citizens not to vote at all than to vote blindly, stupidly.

In ancient Athens—birthplace of democracy and of the idea that voting is a moral duty—it was normal to be informed. Athens was a relatively small city with an intimate sense of community. Issues were right in front of you. If you didn't know a given candidate personally you knew people who did. (Yes, I know, women and slaves couldn't vote, but that's another matter.)

Political Ignorance Is Common

Today, ignorance is all too common. A Léger poll in 2004 showed that 71 per cent of Quebec respondents did not know the name of their MNA [member of the National Assembly, Quebec's legislative body]. The pollster didn't ask about familiarity with the local MP [member of Parliament] and city councillor, but the figures would also have been pathetic.

I'm not suggesting that most voters are dummkopfs. Far from it. The BBM [Canadian TV and radio ratings organization] audience rating for the television debates between party leaders was higher than for typical TV programs. And most voters have a pretty good idea of each party's general orientation (even if each party's program goes largely unread). These citizens—the ones who keep up with the news—do have a moral obligation to vote.

It's the other kind of voter I'm talking about. The kind whose familiarity with a party depends largely on fluff—on posters, for example, or on a candidate's grin. The kind who is a pawn of the herd instinct—"Gee, I heard that the polls show Party X is soaring. I guess I'll vote for it."

There's no gain for a society in getting these people to vote. Their ballots could negate those of people who have actually pondered their choice.

This doesn't mean we ought to shrug at declining voter turnout. Just 58.8 per cent of eligible voters across Canada cast ballots in the last federal election—an alltime low.

In the last Quebec provincial election the turnout was even lower—57.3 per cent, down from 71 per cent in the previous contest. Note, too, that turnouts in Montreal's last two city elections were both sub–40 per cent, the lowest in memory.

It would be nice to think that know-nothing citizens are nobly deciding to abstain from voting for the sake of not risking the election of unfit candidates. But these wilting turnouts are really a reflection of rising apathy toward public affairs. That's the problem that deserves the attention.

More and more people just don't care.

Everyone will have a theory as to why. My own is that the rise of individualism and preoccupation with self-fulfilment are leaving less room for a sense of community, of which a desire to vote is one symptom.

It's silly to implore people who are not interested to vote. It's pointless to try to make them feel guilty if they prefer to watch TV or go to a movie on Monday instead of heading for the polls.

In fact, if they abstain, they're inadvertently doing society a favour.

Let those who give a damn do the voting.

Democracy Does Not Necessarily Promote Individual Autonomy

Jonah Goldberg

Jonah Goldberg, editor at large at the National Review Online, *is the author of* Liberal Fascism *and is a visiting fellow at the American Enterprise Institute, a conservative Washington, DC, think tank.*

The collective understanding of the nature and consequences of democracy and freedom has evolved since Walt Whitman's time. In the following viewpoint, Goldberg states that democracy does not always provide the intended results, as demonstrated by events such as the undemocratic military overthrow of democratic Islamic law in Egypt, which was celebrated in the West, and Palestine's democratic election of Hamas, a group deemed a terrorist organization by the United States. While Goldberg views liberal democracy as an essential component to social order, he perceives the contemporary concept of liberty in the West to have strayed from its original meaning—"free to be us"—to a more selfish notion: "free to be me." Such a change, based in greed and self-interest, he argues, threatens to plunge democracies into dysfunction and chaos.

Finally, the national conversation about democracy is relatively mature and serious. Save for some TV-news anchors, just about everyone seems to understand that democracy is a tricky thing.

That skepticism was hard-earned. The last decade provided painful lessons for everyone, on both sides of the ideo-

Jonah Goldberg, "Liberty, 21st Century–Style," *National Review Online*, February 16, 2011. All rights reserved. Reproduced by permission.

logical aisle. Liberals, who were once naïvely optimistic about democracy promotion, turned dour when President [George W.] Bush became naïvely optimistic about it. And then supporters of Bush's freedom agenda learned a tough lesson from, among other things, the disastrous-but-democratic elections [in 2006] that put a terrorist junta [Hamas] in charge of the Gaza Strip [part of the Palestinian territories].

Hence the irony of so many small-"d" democrats quietly celebrating the fact that Egypt is living under undemocratic martial law, rather than democratic Islamic law as interpreted by a Muslim Brotherhood caliphate.

This new consensus—that democracy is about more than mere lever-pulling on Election Day—is progress.

Democracy is essential to a liberal order, but it is less important than the rule of law, honest courts, individual rights (including property rights), and the institutions—legal and cultural—that nurture them.

George W. Bush famously proclaimed that the desire for freedom burns in every human heart. I'm sympathetic to such notions and the statecraft that drives such pronouncements. But that doesn't get us very far. What drives the urge for liberty?

Personal Liberty Is a New Concept

The notion that we all crave personal liberty is a fairly new one, historically. Most of the calls for freedom over the centuries have been in the context of national, not personal, liberation. The 20th century began with an atrocious war allegedly fought over something called "self-determination," but the "self" in question wasn't the id, ego, or super ego, or the individual soul. The "self" in "self-determination" referred to the captive nations of Europe.

Freedom fighters have generally battled for the collective right to fly a national flag, not the individual right to burn one. Conservatives loved the movie *Braveheart*, with all of its

Mel Gibson as thirteenth-century Scottish nationalist freedom fighter William Wallace in the 1995 film Braveheart. © Frank Trapper/Sygma/Corbis.

beautiful language about freedom, but it's worth remembering that the freedom the Scots fought for was the freedom to replace the authoritarian traditionalism of the English with the authoritarian traditionalism of the Scots.

The great change, as [political scientist] Francis Fukuyama chronicled in his book *The End of History and the Last Man,* has been the evolution of individual self-determination. Fukuyama borrows a term, *thumos,* from the ancient Greeks to explain the transformation. Thumos, or "spiritedness," encompasses the instinct for justice, respect, and integrity.

"People evaluate and assign worth to *themselves* in the first instance, and feel indignation on *their own* behalf," Fukuyama writes. "But they are also capable of assigning worth to *other* people, and feeling anger on behalf of *others.*"

Indignation, the driving passion of all revolutions, shares a root with "dignity," a person's—and a people's—sense of self-worth. A major cause of Middle Eastern political stagnation, for instance, has been that Arab and Muslim dictators have linked their peoples' self-respect with the Palestinians' plight.

More positively, in our own country, the Civil Rights movement and the women's movement were, at their core, what Harvard philosopher Harvey Mansfield calls "honor-seeking movements."

Different Conceptions of "Liberty"

To understand the continuity between the old conception of liberty and the modern one, you need to understand that freedom in the West mostly means "free to be me." Freedom in much of the rest of the world remains "free to be us."

The genius of liberal democracy is that it allows both conceptions to flourish simultaneously, often in healthy tension. Far from perfect, liberal democracy offers the most people the most respect possible.

The tumult in Egypt and throughout the Middle East is a generational conflagration between different conceptions of thumos—old and modern, Muslim and nationalist, collective and individual. In the long run, I'm not too worried about liberal democracy's prospects in the Middle East. Modernity brings prosperity, and prosperity fuels an insatiable appetite for respect, and that demand for respect is what topples tyrannies.

I'm more concerned about what is happening here. Thumos continues to evolve in Western democracies, which is not the same thing as saying it continues to improve.

Our current fiscal woes—not to mention the riot of dysfunction that often goes by the name "political correctness" and the thumos-on-the-cheap that we call the self-esteem industry—are in no small part attributable to the perversion of our sense of self-worth. For millions of Americans, it seems that respect must be paid in the form of cash tribute. How else to explain the inviolable sanctity of our aptly named "entitlement" system?

Great civilizations die when the people believe their personal dignity demands more than the society can possibly provide. Sadly, that conversation has barely begun.

Short-Sighted and Self-Serving Policies Doom Democracies

Randy Salzman

Randy Salzman is a writer and former journalism professor.

In the following viewpoint, Randy Salzman asserts that the financial bailouts of 2008 indicate the failure of democracy in the United States. Special-interest groups, he argues, have realized that by joining together and voting en masse they can siphon money and privileges from the federal government, and such dependence threatens to collapse the economy and eventually the social order. According to Salzman, the founding fathers saw the danger of political policy being beholden to the needs of self-interested individuals or groups and made efforts to foster a sense of mutual sacrifice among the public, but modern-day politicians lack the vision and willpower to demand the same from their constituents.

"A democracy will continue to exist up until the time that voters discover that they can vote themselves generous gifts from the public treasury. From that moment on, the majority always votes for the candidates who promise the most benefits from the public treasury, with the result that every democracy will finally collapse due to loose fiscal policy, which is always followed by a dictatorship. . . ."

"Great nations rise and fall. The people go from bondage to spiritual truth, to great courage, from courage to liberty, from liberty to abundance, from abundance to selfishness, from selfishness to complacency, from complacency to apathy, from apathy to dependence, from dependence back again to bondage."

These words—the author is unknown—are particularly sobering today. In the past few months [in 2008], Uncle Sam has bailed out Wall Street, Fannie Mae and Freddie Mac, home-owners, banks, and US automakers, while the incoming administration promises a massive infrastructure investment.

Is it any surprise that cities, counties, and states are jostling for space at the federal trough? Who's next? Big Media? Big Sports? Agribusiness?

With the bailout "mother of all precedents," it's become difficult for Washington politicians to say "no" to any special interest that's too massive, too economically important, or too well connected to fail.

Nor can politicians forget the poor. Or the crucial swing voters in the "struggling middle class." And they can't ignore seniors—AARP [American Association of Retired Persons] members are very vocal.

Virtually every group today is trying to meet with the [Barack] Obama [presidential] transition team to convey the urgency of its "crucial" spending requests. My local paper recently informed me that our area university is preparing its wish list for infrastructure dollars. Even the National Council for the Social Studies and the American Sportfishing Association have sent pitches to President-elect Obama.

Have Americans Become Complacent?

Have we gone from "rugged individualism" to the complacency or even dependency of the national trajectory quoted above?

At the time of America's founding, the Federalist Papers discussed the dangers of democratic politicians being forced to count on the votes and support of citizens or organizations too self-involved or uneducated to realize that short-term individual or group gain often precludes long-term prosperity.

And Thomas Jefferson sought to deal with politicians' catering to their constituents' convenience by founding the University of Virginia (UVA). He wanted an informed, intelligent, and thoughtful population in hopes of helping democracy survive. Today, sadly, UVA is the area university I read about in the paper seeking funds for its infrastructure wish list.

A century after Jefferson turned UVA's first spade of earth, the 17th Amendment provided for the direct election of US senators, instead of them being beholden to state legislators, as prescribed by the Constitution. Facing John Q. Public every six years instead of legislators, senators began putting their hands out to special interests, and, at that moment, long-term thinking by American government took a massive step backward.

Will Virginia's new senator, Mark Warner (D), for example, feel secure enough to stand on principle and say he can't support UVA's requests?

Senators Rarely Defy Their Constituents

President [John F.] Kennedy's book "Profiles in Courage" recorded only eight incidents in American history when senators stood fast amid the howls of their constituents or party. JFK asked for the best of us, saying pointedly in his inaugural address, "Ask not what your country can do for you—ask what you can do for your country."

Hopefully, we're not sliding toward "final collapse due to loose fiscal policy," but since many of us demand "instant gratification," it may take another inspiring wordsmith to stymie the "me, me, me" cacophony.

Mr. Obama, like Kennedy and Jefferson, is a man with a gilded tongue. Can he lead us to understand that when America races to raid the public treasury, it is, to use a phrase President Lincoln (our greatest leader) borrowed from the Bible, "a house divided against itself"?

Obama says he greatly admires Lincoln. Perhaps he can enjoin all Americans to do now what Lincoln urged during a very different crisis: "If all do not join now to save the good old ship of the Union this voyage, nobody will have a chance to pilot her on another voyage"?

Excessive Individualism Creates Inequality and Weakens America's Social Fabric

D. Stanley Eitzen

D. Stanley Eitzen is professor emeritus of sociology at Colorado State University and the author of such books as Fair and Foul: Beyond the Myths and Paradoxes of Sport.

In the following viewpoint, Eitzen argues that the individualism celebrated by Americans now threatens to tear the country apart. While self-reliance is an admirable credo, he says, people must also realize that concern for the well-being of others makes everyone safer and more prosperous. According to Eitzen, the federal government is in the best position to ensure the well-being of all citizens, but widespread distrust of government programs and institutions—especially under president Barack Obama—has led to legislative gridlock and congressional inaction. Thoughtful political debate and compromise has been replaced by selfish ideological diatribes, which in turn contributes to a widening gap between the haves and the have-nots and increased class, race, and gender strife, all of which threaten the foundations of American democracy.

"We believe that, in a country where every race and faith and point of view can be found, we are still bound together as one people," proclaimed Pres. Barack Obama in his 2011 State of the Union address. Actually, there are at least five societal trends that are weakening the social fabric of our nation: excessive individualism: declining trust in societal institutions; increasing polarization; divides over diversity; and the widening inequality gap.

Americans celebrate individualism. It fits with our economic system of capitalism. We are self-reliant and responsible for our actions. We value individual freedom, including the right to choose our vocations and mates, when and where to travel, and how to spend our money. Rugged individualism, however, has its faults. It promotes inequality: blames the unsuccessful for their failure; shrugs at the existence of inferior housing, schools, and services for "others"; encourages public policies that are punitive to the disadvantaged; and opposes policies for the common good such as public transportation, symphony orchestras, and parks. It exalts private gain over public obligation and special interests over the common good.

The Individualistic Credo Is Flawed

The flaw in the individualistic credo is that we cannot go it alone—our fate depends on others. It is in our individual interest to have a collective interest. We deny this at our peril, for if we allow public squalor and disregard those unlike ourselves, we invite their hostility.

An important ingredient in the stitching that holds society together is trust in institutions. Most fundamentally, people question our economic system when it fails. During the Great Recession, for instance, official unemployment reached more than 10%, while another 6.7% were employed part time but wanted to work full time. Housing values plummeted and the stock market plunged. Clearly, the economic system was misfiring.

The Federal government also is mistrusted by millions of citizens. The birthers believe that Obama cannot hold the office of president because he is not a natural born citizen. Some maintain he is a socialist who is taking the country down a path of destruction. Others fear that the President actually is a Muslim and that he is promoting Islamic power in the world while diminishing the strength of the West.

Questioning Government Legitimacy

With Obama in the White House, Republicans in Congress have tried to stall efforts by the Democrats to pass progressive legislation. This has resulted, for the most part in gridlock. When legislation does pass, such as the health care plan, many object because they feel it is an assault on individual freedoms. Similarly, there were concerns that the government was overreaching when it bailed out the banks and automobile corporations. All of this combined with huge Federal and state debts have left many to question the legitimacy of the present government.

"We are creeping toward an oligarchic society where a relative handful of the rich and privileged decide with their money, who will run, who will win, and how they will govern," claims journalist Bill Moyers. As Robert Reich, former Secretary of Labor, has observed. "It is difficult to represent the little fellow when the big fellow pays the tab." So, instead of a government of, by, and for the people, we have, in the words of Nobel Laureate economist Joseph Stiglitz, a government "of the 1%, by the 1%, and for the 1%."

The role of money in soliciting votes was magnified with the Supreme Court decision allowing organizations unlimited spending on election campaigns. This undermines the unifying myth of American society—"one person, one vote."

Money Controls Politics

Most significant is our collective loss of faith in the political system as a whole. This is because it is controlled by money, while Congress is governed by arcane rules that subvert democracy; there are winner-take-all elections that stifle minorities and gerrymandering of districts to keep in power whichever political party is in the majority; and we choose our president with an electoral college system that gives small states a disproportionate amount of power.

Moreover, public voices, whether in legislatures or the media, have become more shrill and demanding of ideological purity. As the sides coalesce at the extremes, the possibility of consensus, compromise, and civility shrinks. There is a philosophical divide between the two major political parties that has hardened with no room for compromise. For Republicans, government is not the solution to our social problems, it is the problem. Democrats, meanwhile, favor an active government.

Changes in the media have exacerbated polarization. Thirty years ago, there were three broadcast networks. Regardless of which network one chose to watch, news reporting essentially was mainstream and balanced. Now, though—with the advent of cable television, talk radio, political blogs, chat rooms, political magazines, and specialized websites—consumers can select messages that reinforce their beliefs. According to Cass Sunstein, professor of law at Harvard University, when we hear only one side, or are with only like-minded people, soft views tend to harden and become more dogmatic. This phenomenon is called "group polarization." In essence, we have created—and inhabit—a cultural universe tailored to fit our social values and views on political issues. This balkanization is tearing at the fabric of the country.

It is said that we live in a postracial society, as evidenced by the dramatic success of individual minority group members in business education, the arts, entertainment, and sports—as well as the election, for the first time in our history, of an African-American as president. There obviously have been major gains since the civil rights movement of the 1950s and 1960s, but there remains a wide wealth and income gap between whites and minorities. Blacks, for instance, are unemployed at rates that dwarf those of whites—and can anyone truly say our criminal justice system is free of racism?

Increasing Racial Tensions

Demographic changes are increasing racial tensions. American society is becoming more racially and ethnically diverse—a nonwhite majority is expected to pervade by 2042. Many white people especially are concerned about the influx of Latino and Asian immigrants, most notably illegal aliens. "White flight" from diverse neighborhoods is resulting in urban and suburban residential areas and schools becoming more segregated. Fear of the growing numbers of racial and ethnic minorities has led to the growth of white supremacy groups and other hate-mongers. Some vigilante groups even have organized to oversee the Mexican border. Rather than inclusiveness, the mood is one of exclusiveness.

Along with increasing racial and ethnic tensions, there is the question of religious intolerance. Some, most notably Muslims since 9/11, often are the victims of hate crimes and discrimination. There also is widespread intolerance of—and discrimination toward—gays, lesbians, and the transgendered, who are defined as deviants and stigmatized by many members of society as sinful. Politicians often use homosexual and lesbian issues, such as gay marriage, as wedges to divide people into us versus them. Our ever-increasing diversity is a fact of life in U.S. society. The challenge is to shift from building walls to building bridges.

A Growing Wealth Gap

As for finances, in effect, the greater the gap, the greater the injustice. At present, there are the fortunate few, a shrinking middle class, and a larger number of poor and near-poor. We have two tax systems. The one for corporations allows some of the largest earners to escape paying their fair share. In addition, the affluent receive much of their income in capital gains, which is taxed at a lower rate than wages.

The rich are separated from the rest of us. They live in exclusive and safe enclaves, walled off. They play at expensive private clubs while vacationing at the same exclusive resorts, hobnobbing with those of similar economic and social standing. Their families intermarry. Their children go to private schools, interacting with similarly privileged children and avoiding "others."

The poor are segregated as well. They live together in shabby neighborhoods sequestered away from the more affluent. These neighborhoods often are unsafe because of criminal activity and environmental hazards. The poor live in marginal areas and in marginal housing, making them especially vulnerable to floods, hurricanes, and other disasters.

Thus, there is an increasing gap between the haves and have-nots, but it is not just that the "haves" have more money, it is that they appear to be better—that is, they succeed while the poor disproportionately fail. As a result, people are divided into the deserving and undeserving. It seems that if people are labeled as undeserving, then we are justified in not helping them. After all, they are to blame for their failures.

This bias against the poor because they are thought to be undeserving is compounded by the physical separation of the rich from the rest of society. Because the wealthy opt out of public schools and do not utilize public recreation or transportation, they have no reason to invest in and work toward public policies for the good of the whole community. According to sociologist Dalton Conley, the more that Americans have vastly different economic means at their disposal, the harder it is to generate political support for investments that would promote the common good.

"A high degree of inequality causes the comfortable to disavow the needy," maintains economist James K. Galbraith. "It increases the psychological distance separating these groups, making it easier to imagine that defects of character or differences of culture . . . lie behind the separation. [Inequality] is now so wide it threatens, as it did in the Great Depression, the social stability of the country. It has come to undermine our sense of ourselves as a nation of equals. Economic inequality, in this way, challenges the essential unifying myth of American national life."

This gap has resulted in a two-tiered society. Rather than a rising tide lifting all boats, the evidence from the last 30 years is that a rising tide lifts only the yachts.

American Individualism Is Threatened by a Growing Climate of Resentment and Victimization

Peter Goodspeed

Peter Goodspeed is senior reporter for international affairs at the National Post of Toronto.

Self-indulgence and a sense of entitlement, not self-reliance, are to blame for the toxic atmosphere of the American social and political milieu, argues Goodspeed in the following viewpoint. He says that Americans' belief that they, as individuals or as groups united by common interests, are entitled to special treatment by the federal government has led to the spread of a victimhood culture, in which everyone feels they have been wronged by a system rigged in others' favor. In this environment, Goodspeed writes, the mere suggestion of personal sacrifice in the interest of the common good is met with hyperbolic statements comparing moderate political ideas to fascism or communism. It is thus impossible to reach the kinds of compromises that would cure the country's social ills.

The United States is a country filled with complaints. Every day, the rhetoric of crisis, anger and resentment stokes the blast furnaces of talk radio, political television and Internet blogs.

The economy stinks; China is overtaking the United States; the best jobs have gone overseas; living standards are declining; schools are substandard; America is in danger of losing its work ethic, productivity edge, spirit for innovation. . . .

Overwhelming feelings of victimization and a growing sense of entitlement has crept into the American culture. So has the United States been reduced to a nation of whiners?

"The old attitude of self-reliant independence has died. It is not simply that the world has changed, but that Americans have," said Harold Jones, a management professor at Dalton State College in Georgia, who wrote the book *Personal Character and National Destiny*.

One hundred and fifty years ago, English novelist Anthony Trollope travelled down the Mississippi and found people living in sod huts and labouring from dawn to dusk. They had no prospect of immediate improvement in their lives, but they were almost universally optimistic about the future.

America's national character relishes its traditions of egalitarianism, individualism and self-reliance.

"But now, every group that can think of a label for itself presses its claim to special treatment," Prof. Jones said. "We all think we have a right to get more for less effort; we all want to be freed from the burdens of competition; we all want to enlist the government in our cause."

Helplessness Has Replaced Self-Reliance

"The most popular writings 150 years ago were filled with stories of self-reliance, faith, honesty, perseverance and victorious achievement. The modern media, by contrast, careen from one 'crisis' to the next. The emphasis is on helplessness and victimization. Politicians expand their following by offering to 'help' citizens with things they ought to be dealing with themselves."

At the same time, modern American culture has been poisoned by an aggrieved sense of alienation and anger. Compromise is almost impossible in a culture where public debate is driven by celebrities who rely on hysteria to sow division and to increase their own notoriety.

"America once had a culture that fostered respect," said Jim Taylor, an Internet blogger and psychology professor at the University of San Francisco. "Today, the culture to which many Americans are exposed is a purveyor of disrespect. Our sports heroes disrespect their bodies, their sport, their fans. Hip-hop artists rap about violence and misogyny. Celebrities appear to be little more than entitled children.

"Wealth, fame, beauty and inanity are the altar at which too many Americans worship. Reality TV, for example exemplifies everything that is wrong with our society today, promoting greed, dishonesty, humiliation and preoccupation with celebrity, wealth and physical attractiveness.

"It ties in with immediate gratification and the belief that things should be easy for us. There is no expectation of sacrifice."

In 1831, Alexis De Tocqueville, a 26-year-old French aristocrat, spent nine months travelling in the United States and saw an entirely different country.

He sang the praises of an emerging national character that revelled in political freedom and individualism. He relished a frontier spirit that expressed itself in self-reliance, independence and the courage to take risks.

The United States, he said, was a nation that eagerly challenged the impossible.

Apparently, not any more. Self-indulgence seems to have replaced the more traditional American values.

Recently, *New York Times* columnist Thomas Friedman described "a country in a state of incremental decline and losing its competitive edge, because our politics has become just another form of sports entertainment, our Congress a forum for legalized bribery and our main lawmaking institutions divided by toxic partisanship to the point of paralysis."

Wall Street's Self-Indulgence

Less than a year after the nation's financial leaders were bailed out by government, U.S. executives have reeled in anger at suggestions they should temporarily limit their bonuses.

That resentment careened toward the ridiculous this summer [2010], when Stephen Schwarzman, the billionaire head of the Blackstone Group, compared a proposal by U.S. President Barack Obama to tax the earnings of private equity and hedge fund managers at the same rate as other workers' income to "when Hitler invaded Poland in 1939."

Last month [September 2010], at a town hall meeting with Mr. Obama, one of his former Harvard Law School classmates, hedge fund billionaire Anthony Scaramucci, indignantly demanded to know, "When are we going to stop whacking at the Wall Street piñata?"

Democratic party activists are so badly infected with this malady they now appear to be entering next month's [November 2010] Congressional elections in a state of indolent indifference, upset with Mr. Obama and the Democratic Congress for failing to give them enough over the last two years.

That elicited a stern upbraiding by Mr. Obama, in a recent *Rolling Stone* magazine interview, when he insisted it is "just irresponsible" and "inexcusable" for his supporters to sit on their hands in the coming elections.

"People need to shake off this lethargy. People need to buck up," he said.

U.S. Vice-President Joe Biden, exasperated with Democrats who believe they are going to be pummelled at the polls in November, last week told a group of New Hampshire donors they "should remind our base constituency to stop whining and get out there and look at the alternatives."

The United States has become a battleground for class warfare between the haves and have-nots, instead of a land of opportunity.

A Government in Gridlock

In the process, government has skidded into gridlock, and polarization and wrangling dominate debate.

A tax revolt rally sponsored by the Tea Party on tax day, April 15, 2010, at the Washington Monument in Washington, DC. © AP Images/Haley/Sipa.

The Tea Party movement, a grass roots protest against government growth and the deficit, is a reaction to this.

Jill Lepore, a Harvard University historian and author of *The Whites of Their Eyes*, a new book on the Tea Party, said the movement represents a shift toward "historical fundamentalism."

"The central assumption of this historical fundamentalism is that the founding documents are sacred and the founding fathers were divinely inspired," she said.

That inserts an absolutism into political discussions that makes any debate difficult.

"There is a discomfort with the complexity of what the country is. There is this sort of atavistic feeling on the far right, where we look to the past for our values, because the present is somehow so abhorrent," she said. "There is a nostalgia for a time when there was unity or singleness of purpose."

"We have lost the road to the national vision," Dr. Taylor said. "There is much more emotion in politics than there used to be and people are driven by fear and anger."

U.S. society has become overwhelmingly adversarial, said Deborah Tannen, a linguistics professor at Georgetown University.

"The war on drugs, the battle of the sexes, politicians' turf battles—war metaphors pervade our talk and shape our thinking," she writes in her book *The Argument Culture: America's War of Words*.

However, Michael Ledeen, a scholar at the Foundation for Defending Democracies and author of the book *Tocqueville: On American Character*, dismissed talk of a transformation of U.S. national character.

"What we are going through now is simple American fractiousness and going at each other," he said.

In 1831, De Tocqueville himself recognized that the U.S. national character was riddled with contradictions, Dr. Ledeen said.

"Those inner contradictions are constant. It's where our energy comes from," he argued. "We simultaneously believe that the most important thing in life is religion and the most important thing in life is money. We believe them both at the same time and we believe in rugged individualism and that we should always be helping other people in whatever way we can.

"Anyone who tries to slap a simple label on us has missed the whole point."

Individuals Have More Opportunities than Ever Before

Thomas L. Friedman

Thomas L. Friedman is a Pulitzer Prize–winning journalist and author whose works include the best-selling book The World Is Flat: A Brief History of the Twenty-First Century.

In the following viewpoint, Friedman employs two opposing concepts, the "Great Disruption" and the "Big Shift" theories, to explain the rise of social unrest around the world in the twenty-first century. The Great Disruption theory, put forth by author Paul Gilding, views social movements like Occupy Wall Street as signs that the current democratic capitalist system has failed the majority of citizens and is collapsing on itself. The Big Shift theory, proposed by John Hagel III, posits that recent developments in technology have created a new, globalized economy that makes old institutions obsolete, resulting in a period of contraction and stress but also innovation and collaboration. Friedman agrees with Hagel but finds an element of ominous truth in Gilding's notion of the Great Disruption.

When you see spontaneous social protests erupting from Tunisia to Tel Aviv to Wall Street, it's clear that something is happening globally that needs defining. There are two unified theories out there that intrigue me. One says this is the start of "The Great Disruption." The other says that this is all part of "The Big Shift." You decide.

The Great Disruption

Paul Gilding, the Australian environmentalist and author of the book "The Great Disruption," argues that these demon-

This April 13, 2012, photograph shows Occupy Movement protesters camping overnight on the corner of Wall Street near the New York Stock Exchange. © Stephanie Keith/Demotix/ Corbis.

strations are a sign that the current growth-obsessed capitalist system is reaching its financial and ecological limits. "I look at the world as an integrated system, so I don't see these protests, or the debt crisis, or inequality, or the economy, or the climate going weird, in isolation—I see our system in the painful process of breaking down," which is what he means by the Great Disruption, said Gilding. "Our system of economic growth, of ineffective democracy, of overloading planet earth—our system—is eating itself alive. Occupy Wall Street is like the kid in the fairy story saying what everyone knows but is afraid to say: the emperor has no clothes. The system is broken. Think about the promise of global market capitalism. If we let the system work, if we let the rich get richer, if we let corporations focus on profit, if we let pollution go unpriced and unchecked, then we will all be better off. It may not be equally distributed, but the poor will get less poor, those who work hard will get jobs, those who study hard will get better jobs and we'll have enough wealth to fix the environment."

"What we now have—most extremely in the U.S. but pretty much everywhere—is the mother of all broken promises," Gilding adds. "Yes, the rich are getting richer and the corporations are making profits—with their executives richly rewarded. But, meanwhile, the people are getting worse off—drowning in housing debt and/or tuition debt—many who worked hard are unemployed; many who studied hard are unable to get good work; the environment is getting more and more damaged; and people are realizing their kids will be even worse off than they are. This particular round of protests may build or may not, but what will not go away is the broad coalition of those to whom the system lied and who have now woken up. It's not just the environmentalists, or the poor, or the unemployed. It's most people, including the highly educated middle class, who are feeling the results of a system that saw all the growth of the last three decades go to the top 1 percent."

The Big Shift

Not so fast, says John Hagel III, who is the co-chairman of the Center for the Edge at [financial consultancy firm] Deloitte, along with John Seely Brown. In their recent book, "The Power of Pull," they suggest that we're in the early stages of a "Big Shift," precipitated by the merging of globalization and the Information Technology Revolution. In the early stages, we experience this Big Shift as mounting pressure, deteriorating performance and growing stress because we continue to operate with institutions and practices that are increasingly dysfunctional—so the eruption of protest movements is no surprise.

Yet, the Big Shift also unleashes a huge global flow of ideas, innovations, new collaborative possibilities and new market opportunities. This flow is constantly getting richer and faster. Today, they argue, tapping the global flow becomes the key to productivity, growth and prosperity. But to tap this flow effectively, every country, company and individual needs to be constantly growing their talents.

"We are living in a world where flow will prevail and topple any obstacles in its way," says Hagel. "As flow gains momentum, it undermines the precious knowledge stocks that in the past gave us security and wealth. It calls on us to learn faster by working together and to pull out of ourselves more of our true potential, both individually and collectively. It excites us with the possibilities that can only be realized by participating in a broader range of flows. That is the essence of the Big Shift."

Problems, but Also Problem Solvers

Yes, corporations now have access to more cheap software, robots, automation, labor and genius than ever. So holding a job takes more talent. But the flip side is that individuals—*individuals*—anywhere can now access the flow to take online courses at Stanford from a village in Africa, to start a new company with customers everywhere or to collaborate with people anywhere. We have more big problems than ever and more problem-solvers than ever.

So there you have it: Two master narratives—one threat-based, one opportunity-based, but both involving seismic changes. Gilding is actually an optimist at heart. He believes that while the Great Disruption is inevitable, humanity is best in a crisis, and, once it all hits, we will rise to the occasion and produce transformational economic and social change (using tools of the Big Shift). Hagel is also an optimist. He knows the Great Disruption may be barreling down on us, but he believes that the Big Shift has also created a world where more people than ever have the tools, talents and potential to head it off. My heart is with Hagel, but my head says that you ignore Gilding at your peril.

You decide.

For Further Discussion

1. Walt Whitman radically altered his writing style in the 1850s, developing what came to be known as free verse, in order to better communicate his ideas about the role of the individual in American society to an increasingly diverse readership. In what ways have artists, politicians, and other public figures adapted their methods of communication in recent years to reach the widest possible audience?

2. As George Kateb points out in Chapter 2, Whitman's concept of the individual—exemplified by the "I" persona of *Leaves of Grass*—was closely related to his understanding of society as a whole. What aspects of life in the nineteenth century might have led him to stress the interdependence of the individual and society? Can the same claims be made about the relationship between the individual and society today? Why or why not?

3. C.K. Williams suggests in Chapter 2 that Whitman strove to make his poetry as distinctly American as possible. What images, ideas, or words in Whitman's poetry strike you as being unique to the American experience? Explain your answers.

4. The essays by Michael Frank and Eric Conrad in Chapter 2 imply that the commonly held images of Whitman—either as a reclusive dreamer or an affable wanderer who opposed discrimination in any form—may in fact be the products of an extensive public relations campaign on the part of his publishers and enthusiastic readers. Should Whitman's poetry and legacy be reevaluated in the light of new discoveries about his true feelings toward slavery,

gender equality, and democracy? Would his poetry have had the same impact if the details of his personal life had been public knowledge during his lifetime? Explain.

5. Despite his faith in democracy, Whitman was notoriously skeptical of government officials and was even fired from a government job due to his controversial statements in *Leaves of Grass*. D. Stanley Eitzen maintains in Chapter 3 that a lack of trust in the federal government threatens to destroy any semblance of unity in the contemporary United States. Can a democracy function without a strong central government? Why or why not?

6. Jonah Goldberg argues in Chapter 3 that, while in Whitman's time democracy allowed countries like the United States the freedom to express their unique national character through a representative government, it has since evolved into a power struggle between narrow-minded special interests and often produces results that benefit only a small portion of the population. Would any other form of government be better suited to address the needs of all citizens, or has the United States become so diverse and fragmented that every policy decision is bound to leave some segments dissatisfied? Explain.

For Further Reading

Frederick Douglass, *Narrative of the Life of Frederick Douglass, an American Slave.* 1845.

Ralph Waldo Emerson, "Politics," in *Essays: Second Series.* 1844.

James Russell Lowell, *Biglow Papers.* 1867.

———, *Democracy and Other Addresses.* 1886.

Herman Melville, *Battle-Pieces and Other Aspects of War.* 1866.

Henry David Thoreau, *Collected Poems.* Ed. Carl Bode. 1964.

Walt Whitman, *Democratic Vistas.* 1871.

———, *Drum-Taps.* 1865.

———, *Franklin Evans; or, the Inebriate.* 1842.

———, *Leaves of Grass.* 1st ed. 1855.

———, *Leaves of Grass.* 9th ed. 1892.

———, *Memoranda During the War.* 1875.

Bibliography

Books

Gay Wilson Allen and Ed Folsom, eds. *Walt Whitman and the World.* Iowa City: University of Iowa Press, 1995.

Harold Bloom, ed. *Walt Whitman.* Philadelphia: Chelsea House, 2003.

Angus Fletcher *A New Theory for American Poetry: Democracy, the Environment, and the Future of Imagination.* Cambridge, MA: Harvard University Press, 2004.

Ezra Greenspan, ed. *The Cambridge Companion to Walt Whitman.* New York: Cambridge University Press, 1993.

Donald D. Kummings, ed. *A Companion to Walt Whitman.* Malden, MA: Blackwell, 2006.

Stephen John Mack *The Pragmatic Whitman: Reimagining American Democracy.* Iowa City: University of Iowa Press, 2002.

Alan Marshall *American Experimental Poetry and Democratic Thought.* New York: Oxford University Press, 2009.

Robert K. Martin, ed. *The Continuing Presence of Walt Whitman: The Life After the Life.* Iowa City: University of Iowa Press, 1992.

Robert Pinsky
Democracy, Culture, and the Voice of Poetry. Princeton, NJ: Princeton University Press, 2002.

Alessandro Portelli
The Text and the Voice: Writing, Speaking, and Democracy in American Literature. New York: Columbia University Press, 1994.

David S. Reynolds
Walt Whitman's America: A Cultural Biography. New York: Knopf, 1995.

John E. Seery, ed.
A Political Companion to Walt Whitman. Lexington: University Press of Kentucky, 2011.

Edward L. Widmer
Young America: The Flowering of Democracy in New York City. New York: Oxford University Press, 1999.

Periodicals and Internet Sources

Eric Alterman
"The Twilight of Social Democracy," *Nation*, August 1–8, 2011.

Conrad Black
"A Great Country That Could Be Better," *National Review Online*, July 13, 2010. www.nationalreview.com.

Jorge Luis Borges
"Walt Whitman, Poet of Democracy," *Commonweal*, May 22, 1981.

Demetrios James Caraley
"Complications of American Democracy: Elections Are Not Enough," *Political Science Quarterly*, vol. 120, no. 3, 2005.

J.M. Coetzee
"Love and Walt Whitman," *New York Review of Books*, September 22, 2005.

Joannie Fischer   "Those Rugged Individuals," *U.S. News & World Report*, June 28, 2004.

Jason Frank   "Aesthetic Democracy: Walt Whitman and the Poetry of the People," *Review of Politics*, June 2007.

Francis Fukuyama   "Is the Age of Democracy Over?" *Spectator*, February 13, 2010.

David Graeber   "Occupy and Anarchism's Gift of Democracy," *Guardian* (Manchester, UK), November 15, 2011.

Michael Ignatieff   "Who Are Americans to Think That Freedom Is Theirs to Spread?" *New York Times*, June 26, 2005.

Joann P. Krieg   "Democracy in Action: Naming the Bridge for Walt Whitman," *Walt Whitman Quarterly Review*, vol. 12, no. 2, 1994.

Richard Rahn   "Liberty vs. Democracy," *Washington Times*, February 6, 2006.

Louis A. Ruprecht   "Walt Whitman's Sacred Democracy," *Religion Dispatches*, January 9, 2011.

Jim Scofield   "The Poet of American Democracy," *Johnstown (PA) Tribune-Democrat*, December 12, 2008.

Greg Smith   "Whitman, Springsteen, and the American Working Class," *Midwest Quarterly*, Spring 2000.

Kathleen Kennedy Townsend   "Walt Whitman and the Soul of Democracy," *Atlantic*, July 8, 2011.

Index

CPSIA information can be obtained
at www.ICGtesting.com
Printed in the USA
FFOW01n1046180516
24191FF

9 780737 763782